Fortune:

"All is but Fortune"

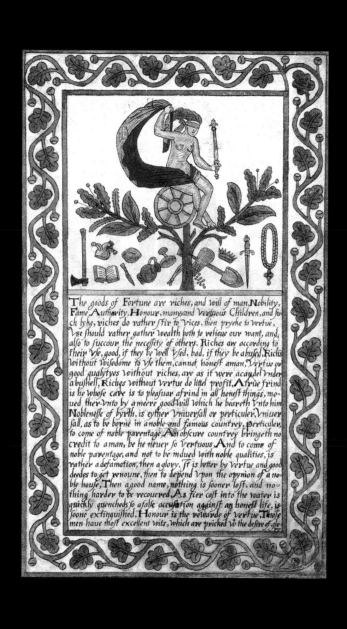

The goods of Fortune are riches, and will of man, Nobility,
Fame, Authority, Honour, many and Vertuous Children, and such
ch lyke, riches do rather stir to vices, then pryeke to vertue,
Vse should rather gather wealth both to relieue our want, and,
also to succour the necessity of others. Riches are according to
their Vse, good, if they be well vsed, bad, if they be abused, Riches
without wisedome to vse them, cannot honest a man, vertue or
good qualytyes without riches, are as it were a candel vnder
a bushell, Riches without vertue do littel profit, A true frind
is he whose care is to pleasuar a frind in all honest things, mo-
ued ther vnto by a meere good will which he beareth vnto him
Noblenesse of byrth, is eyther vniuersall or perticuler, vniuersall, as to be borne in a noble and famous countrey, perticuler,
to come of noble parentage, An obscure countrey bringeth no
credit to a man, be he neuer so vertuous, And to come of
noble parentage, and not to be indued with noble qualities, is
rather a defamation, then a glory, It is better by vertue and good
deedes to get renoune, then to depend vpon the opynion of a noble house, Then a good name, nothing is sooner lost, and nothing harder to be recouered, As fier cast into the water is
quickly quencheds so a false accusation against an honest life, is
soone extinguished, Honour is the rewarde of vertue, Those
men haue most excellent wits, which are pricked vt the desire of glo-

Fortune:

"All is but Fortune"

Compiled and edited
by Leslie Thomson

The Folger Shakespeare Library
Washington, D.C., 2000

Distributed by
University of Washington Press
Seattle and London

This volume has been published in conjunction
with the exhibition *Fortune: "All is but Fortune,"*
presented at the Folger Shakespeare Library,®
Washington, D.C., from January 18 through
June 10, 2000.

Werner Gundersheimer, Director.

Richard Kuhta, Librarian.

Rachel Doggett, Andrew W. Mellon Curator
of Books and Exhibitions.

The exhibition and the catalogue have been
funded by The Winton and Carolyn Blount
Exhibitions Fund and the Andrew W. Mellon
Publications Fund of the Folger Library.

Distributed by
the University of Washington Press,
Seattle and London.
ISBN 0–295-97967-4

Photographs by Julie Ainsworth.

Frontispiece: *Fortuna*, from Thomas Trevelyon,
Pictorial commonplace book, Manuscript, 1608.

Design by Studio A, Alexandria, Virginia

Printing by Hagerstown Bookbinding
and Printing, Hagerstown, Maryland

Contents

Foreword

It would be easy to take a dismissive stance towards so traditional a concept as the idea of fortune. After all, fortune conceived as a model for explaining a world filled with unpredictable outcomes seemed superficial and passé even in the time of Saint Augustine (c. 400). He proposed Divine Providence as the determining agent in human affairs, thus replacing the classical notions of random events and endlessly recurrent cycles with a foreordained plan subsuming the vicissitudes of earthly events to a Last Judgment awaiting all creatures at the end of time. Augustine's powerful model, which met the great intellectual test of imposing a pattern on what had seemed for centuries to be beyond explaining, struck a blow at the idea of fortune.

But Fortune never died. Throughout the medieval centuries, the fickle goddess survived in all sorts of literary and artistic sources, ready to be appropriated in traditional as well as innovative ways by the artists and writers of early modern Europe. Even if the original Greek and Roman representations of Tyche or Fortuna had gone undiscovered by the Italian humanists, the goddess— together with her many attributes—would have remained available as a traditional means of interpreting the flux. Political thinkers like Machiavelli invoked her, but so did physicians, playwrights, printers, painters, pamphleteers, even philosophers.

Yet, perhaps something more than antiquarian curiosity, that worthy motivator, has driven the erudite and imaginative curator of this exhibition, Professor Leslie Thomson, of the University of Toronto, to discover the vast array of allusions to fortune embedded in the Folger's books and manuscripts. For on the cusp of a new millennium, the human species, which has lately devised and/or discovered explanations for most of the phenomena which puzzled earlier generations, still struggles with the opacities of chance. Consider, for example, the furious debates waged over the premises of sociobiology, which could be regarded as the modern scientist's version of Divine Providence. Can it be that our outcomes, far from being random and unpredictable, are foretold in our genetic sequencing? And what, if anything, determines that? What about viral mutations, the weird turnabouts that affect the lottery of this year's flu shot, or next year's tuberculosis epidemic? Aren't they, in some sense, Fortuna operating at the molecular level?

To peruse this exhibition and to read and ponder this catalogue is to confront the perennial insecurity of our race. We humans seem unique among the animals in our capacity to worry about what we cannot fully control. All of us live with doubt and fear. For some, the dread becomes pathological. Are there creatures in outer space? Will the earth be assaulted by meteors or burnt up by gamma rays? Does a new millennium prefigure some great cataclysm? Do I dare to live near the San Andreas Fault? Do I dare to eat a peach? Will this plane fly? Whence these oysters? And so on. There is, then, a close kinship between the fortune-obsessed inhabitants of early modern Europe and their anxiety-ridden modern counterparts of the nuclear age. That kinship, as Leslie Thomson shows, goes beyond the shared symptoms of malaise, for it includes the mental constructs, the visual and verbal vocabularies with which we try to come to terms with our hopes and fears in an uncertain world. Like our European antecedents, we embrace unpromising strategies to make things come out right—touch wood, skip the thirteenth floor, watch out for that black cat (the Devil, another medieval and Renaissance terror), say "break a leg," call it "the Scottish play," blow on our dice, play our mother's birthdate on the Powerball. In learning, through *Fortune: "All is but Fortune,"* how early modern people saw their world, leave your condescension at the door. They do, indeed, hold up a distant mirror for ourselves.

Werner Gundersheimer
Director

Introduction
Fortune: "All is but Fortune"

Leslie Thomson, *University of Toronto*

The phrase "all is but Fortune" (*The Tempest* 5.1) expresses both the hope and the resignation that characterize the Renaissance attitude to Fortune illustrated and examined in this catalogue and in the exhibition that it documents. The idea that Fortune is in control is one we can still understand because the realities and questions personified by the emblematic figure of *Fortuna* are much the same today as they were four hundred years ago. Arbitrary change in the world is the same; unjust reward and punishment, unwarranted success and failure are still inexplicable. The sense that we have limited power to control events and the problem of individual freedom versus necessity both remain as troubling for us as they were for Seneca, Boethius, Shakespeare, Machiavelli, and Bacon, to name only some of those quoted here. Fortune has evolved from classical goddess, to Renaissance personification, to a much looser modern concept; but while we no longer believe in the goddess, or depict Fortune in emblems, we are still very much aware that our world is, or seems to be, a realm governed by chance and mutability. Out of this fact grow questions about whether we are responsible for our own bad fortune—the good we usually accept as our due—and how we can avoid misfortune in the future. The desire to control the turning of Fortune's

wheel is as strong as ever: astrology, palmistry, and other forms of "fortune telling"—even market forecasting and political polls—are attempts to know and determine the future.

Representations of Fortune from classical antiquity to the late Renaissance in England and on the Continent are the main focus of this catalogue. In the evolution of the depiction of Fortune over this period of time it is possible to see how the idea itself changes. In particular, Fortune's dominance becomes apparent in illustrations that show her with the accoutrements of *Nemesis* and, especially, *Occasio*, two goddesses with related but significantly different powers. The idea that Fortune can be controlled, implied by this conflation, is an important aspect of this study since it is an idea found not only in illustrations but in literature as well. Indeed, Fortune is a central element of many plays, poems, and prose works throughout the Renaissance, which the Folger Library's wide collection makes it possible to bring together here.

Belief in a goddess of Fortune who controls human events had its origins in classical antiquity, but Christianity countered the idea with the assertion that Providence governed all worldly events. The argument of Christianity was that ignorance of God's plan led humans to try to explain the inex-

plicable by creating a goddess whose primary quality and function was random change. The resulting conflict between the reality of everyday experience and the belief in a governing order finds expression in the images and words of artists who, by virtue of what they do, can be said to be trying to control Fortune by the delimiting methods of art. Not surprisingly, times of great change engender a more acute awareness and wariness of the vagaries of Fortune. The fifteenth, sixteenth, and seventeenth centuries were characterized by economic and social change determined largely by the exploration, discovery, and development of "new worlds," both domestic and foreign, metaphoric and literal. The sense of being subject not to an ultimately benevolent Providence but to fickle Fortune's always turning wheel was understandably vivid. Then there was a receptive audience for attempts to illustrate and explain the vicissitudes of life in a mutable world; today, as we look toward a new millennium and are especially conscious of being subject to time and change in an unpredictable universe, I hope that this exhibition and catalogue will engender a similar interest.

The breadth and depth of the Folger Library's collection, which goes far beyond Shakespeare, has made it possible for me to

put together the exhibition and catalogue. The idea to have an exhibition on Fortune as 2000 begins seems almost inevitable now. But the project actually evolved over some years out of a passing remark I was fortunate, or unfortunate, enough to make to Rachel Doggett, the Folger's curator of exhibitions, that given its resources the Library should do such an exhibition. And my awareness of Fortune's potential as a topic has origins even further back, in an undergraduate course on early English drama and in a graduate seminar on the epic, both taught at the University of Toronto by a truly inspiring professor, Peter Marinelli. That he died in 1993 at the age of fifty-nine is a sad instance of fickle Fortune's ways. The exhibition is very much a tribute to his expertise and enthusiasm, only the second of which I can hope to emulate. For help with my rudimentary knowledge of the many aspects of Fortune's origins and development I have relied especially on Frederick Kiefer's invaluable study, *Fortune and Elizabethan Tragedy* (1983), and on Samuel Chew's *The Pilgrimage of Life* (1962); without these essential works, I could not have hoped to acquire the knowledge necessary even to begin my exploration of the Folger collections. Other studies of Fortune and related topics on which I have depended, often to the point of paraphrase,

are cited through the catalogue. Because studies of Fortune in English are relatively few, and I know from experience what it is to want more, this catalogue also includes essays by four scholars, each of whom has explored an aspect of Fortune so as to offer some particular applications of the more general information provided in the catalogue. We hope that the two approaches will be mutually illuminating.

I am grateful to Werner Gundersheimer, Director of the Folger Shakespeare Library, and Richard Kuhta, Librarian, for their initial and continuing interest in this project. Special thanks are due to Rachel Doggett, Andrew W. Mellon Curator of Books and Exhibitions, whose encouragement, expertise, and energy brought the exhibition and catalogue into being. Without the almost constant and always efficient assistance of the Reading Room staff, especially Betsy Walsh and Susan Sehulster, my research would not have been possible. I very much appreciate the contributions of conservators Frank Mowery, Linda Blaser, Julie Biggs, and Linda Hohneke, photographer Julie Ainsworth, and registrar Andy Tennant. For his enthusiasm about the project, for his many practical suggestions, and for his translations, I offer warm thanks to John Astington, to whom I am also grateful, along with Judith Dundas,

Frederick Kiefer, and Alan Young, for their thoughtful and pertinent essays. I am also indebted to Robert Iorillo, who provided many translations of Latin and Greek, Eve Sanders, who helped with French, and Julie Biggs and Werner Gundersheimer, who helped with Italian. For their assistance and willingness to provide a number of important items without which the exhibition and catalogue would be less than they are, I thank the National Gallery of Art and curators Alison Luchs and C. Douglas Lewis, Jr.; I also want to thank the Museum of American History, Smithsonian Institution, and curator David Shayt of the Division of Cultural History.

The image reproduced on page 2 is from Thomas Trevelyon's pictorial commonplace book (1608), a unique color manuscript of pictures and text covering a variety of subjects, including alphabets, the calendar, medicine, astrology, monarchs, and allegorical figures like this one. The drawing of Fortune incorporates virtually all the accoutrements typically associated with her: wheel, sail, blindfold, sceptre, and tree. Below the goddess are the things of the world. The text emphasizes that Virtue is necessary if these goods are to be used in the service of the Good.

AGTVS QVINTI: SCENA PRIMA.

Rinaldo solus.

Fortune the great commandresse of the world,
Hath diuers wayes to aduance her followers:
To some she giues honour without deseruing,
To other some deseruing without honour,
Some wit, some wealth : and some wit without wealth:
Some wealth without wit, some, nor wit nor wealth

I.

Classical Origins

"By the grumbling of men Fortune is made a goddess."

(Publius Syrus, *Sententiae*, no. 180, c. 43 B.C.)

The word *fortuna* is from the Latin *fors*, or "luck," derived from the root of the verb *ferre* ("to bring"), so that the meaning is "that which is brought," and *Fortuna* is the one who brings it. The related Greek figure is *Tyche*, whose name is based on a root word meaning "to succeed" or "to attain," implying something more positive than mere chance. The figure depicted in Roman art is *Fortuna Gubernans*, the helmsman; or *Fortuna stabilis*, with the appropriate attributes—rudder or wheel—shown at rest. But classical satire was not so complacent, characterizing *Fortuna* as inconstant and fickle, more like the figure of the Renaissance. The Roman goddess brought *bona fortunae*, external goods such as wealth, health, power, progeny, and physical beauty—all things that are vulnerable to good and bad fortune. In pagan antiquity *Fortuna* was thought to be the ruler of human life, but at the same time it was asserted that people could control their fortune by such personal qualities as virtue, prudence, and courage. Aristotle's argument that chance was a necessary condition for the exercise of free will was the foundation of this seemingly contradictory idea. Cicero believed that reason could be used to control Fortune, as illustrated in this passage from his *De Officiis* (44 B.C.):

Who fails to comprehend the enormous, two-fold power of Fortune for weal and for woe? When we enjoy her favouring breeze, we are wafted over to the wished-for haven; when she blows against us, we are dashed to destruction. Fortune herself, then, does send those other less usual calamities, arising, first, from inanimate Nature—hurricanes, storms, shipwrecks, catastrophes, conflagrations; second, from wild beasts—kicks, bites, and attacks. But these, as I have said, are comparatively rare. But think, on the one side, of the destruction of armies…, the loss of generals…, the hatred of the masses, too, and the banishment that as a consequence frequently comes to men of eminent services, their degration and voluntary exile; think, on the other hand, of the successes, the civil and military honours, and the victories;—though all these contain an element of chance, still they cannot be brought about, whether for good or for ill, without the cooperation of our fellow-men. With this understanding of the influence of Fortune, I may proceed to explain how we can win the affectionate cooperation of our fellows and enlist it in our service.[1]

Somewhat later Pliny, in his *Historia Naturalis* (c. 77) criticized those who blamed Fortune for all human events in terms that would reappear in Renaissance literature, philosophy, and art:

Everywhere in the whole world at every hour by all men's voices Fortune alone is invoked and named, alone accused, alone impeached, alone pondered, alone applauded, alone rebuked and visited with reproaches; deemed volatile and indeed by most men blind as well, wayward, inconstant, uncertain, fickle in her favours and favouring the unworthy. To her is debited all that is spent and credited all that is received, she alone fills both pages in the whole of mortals' account; and we are so much at the mercy of chance that Chance herself, by whom God is proved uncertain, takes the place of God.[2]

Opposite left: Printer's device of Thomas Marsh in Richard Carew, *A Herrings Tayle*, London, 1598.

Opposite right: From George Chapman, *All Fooles*, London, 1605.

2

3

The Renaissance fascination with all things classical led antiquaries not only to collect the art and artifacts of the Greek and Roman worlds but also to describe, study, and illustrate the materials they collected.

1.
Giovanni Battista Cavalleriis
Antiquarum Statuarum urbis Romae
Rome, 1585–1594
No. 13: "Fortunae imago marmorca in uiridario Vaticano": "The marble statue of Fortune in the pleasure garden of the Vatican"

Renaissance interest in classical Rome resulted in numerous books such as this one about the collecting of antiquities. Here Fortune is a positive figure, as the Romans imagined her: clothed and holding a cornucopia, one of her earliest accoutrements.

2.
François Antoine Pomey
Pantheum Mythicum
Utrecht, 1697
Page 295

This too is Fortune as the Romans imagined her: clothed, with a rudder, cornucopia, and headpiece. The medals at the top depict the goddess in various classical manifestations. Pomey's handbook of classical mythology reproduces the reverses of coins and medals whose images of gods and goddesses were studied and interpreted by Renaissance scholars.

3.
Niccolò Fiorentino
Fortune with rudder and cornucopia
Archbishop of Florence on obverse
Medal, bronze
National Gallery of Art

Samuel H. Kress Collection (1957.14.855b) "Bene facere et letari" and "Fort[una] red[ux]": "Fare well and be happy" and "Fortune brought back"

The medal may commemorate the return of Rinaldo Orsini, Archbishop of Florence (1474–1510), from Rome to Florence in 1485.[3]

4.
Bernard de Montfaucon
L'Antiquité Expliquée
Paris, 1722
Vol. 2, part 1, no. 19: The Temple of Fortune at Praeneste

The Temple of Fortune is described in the English translation of Pomey, *The Pantheon, representing the fabulous histories of the heathen gods and most illustrious heroes:* "Her Temple at *Praeneste,* from whence she was called *Praenestina,* was famouser, and more spoken of than all the rest; by reason, there were very true *Oracles* uttered there."[4]

5.
Richard Linche
The Fountaine of Ancient Fiction
Derived from Vincenzo Cartari, *Le imagini de i dei de gli antichi*
London, 1599
Sigs. Z2v–Z3r

In this work, written in Italian and translated into English, numerous classical sources are referred to and quoted, here about Roman concepts of *Fortuna.* The temple at Praeneste was "dedicated vnto Fortune, wherein was drawne out & portrayed a Picture or Image in the shape and forme of two Sisters, both conioned together in the same Statue, and that it was there held and worshipped in high reuerence and adoration." Cartari then lists and explains the attributes of classical Fortune.

6.
Ben Jonson
Sejanus
London, 1605
Sigs. K3v–K4r
See Kiefer, fig. 5

Jonson's play about the fall of a Roman consul includes a scene drawn from history in which a statue of Fortune is worshipped:

Great mother Fortvne, Queene of humane
*   state,*
Rectresse of Action, Arbitresse of Fate,
To whom all sway, all power, all empire bowes,
Be present, and propitious to our vowes.

As a ceremony of propitiation is performed, the statue begins to move: "See, see, the Image stirres," says Terentius, and Satrius replies, "And turnes away." They seem not to realize that prayers to Fortune are useless because her acts are random. The marginal annotations are Jonson's, giving his classical sources for these events.

"That which Fortune has not given,
she cannot take away."
(Seneca, *Epistulae ad Lucilium*,
Epis. lix, sec. 18)

The Stoics understood that *Fortuna* could not easily be controlled and adopted the position that the way to endure life's ups and downs was simply to accept them by realizing that although we cannot control our fortune, we can control our response to it. A further development of this position can be found in the work of Seneca, who argued that because ambition and high place seem to attract bad fortune, the ideal is a life of moderation, of adherence to the Golden Mean.

7.
Seneca
Seneca His Tenne Tragedies
London, 1581
Page 92

A sixteenth-century translation by Alexander Neville of Seneca's play *Oedipus* mixes the stoicism of the original with a hint of later attitudes. The Chorus at the end of the fourth act focuses on the idea of control from above by "fatal fates":

What mankind bydes or does on earth it
*   cometh from aboue,*
Then wayling grones powrd out in griefe
*   do nought at all behoue.*
Our life must haue her pointed course, (alas)
*   what shall I say:*
As fates decree, so things do run, no man
*   can make them stay.*
For at our byrth to Gods is known our latter
*   dying day.*
No Prayer, no Arte, not God himselfe may
*   fatall fates resist.*
But fastned all in fixed course, unchaunged
*   they persist.*
Such ende them still ensues as they appointed
*   were to haue,*
Than fly all feare of Fortunes chaung, seeke
*   not to lyue a slave*
Enthrald in bondage vyle to feare. For feare
*   doth often bring*
Destinies that dreaded ben and mischiefs
*   feard upon us fling.*

Another response, one which fed directly into Christianity, was that of *contemptu mundi* ("contempt of the world"), based on the view that life in the world of time is only a temporary condition and that the eternal afterlife is what really matters. The most famous and influential exponent of this view was Boethius, in his *Consolation of Philosophy* (524). Although not explicitly Christian, it certainly expresses the position of Christianity that human life is ruled not by Fortune but by Providence. A benevolent force, Providence ensures that in fact all fortune is good fortune, even if it does not seem so to humans, who have a limited knowledge of the divine. With Boethius we move from the classical to the medieval world.

HVLDERICHI

HVTTENI EQ. GERM.
DIALOGI.

FORTVNA.
Febris prima.
Febris secunda
Trias Romana.
Inspicientes.

Cum priuilegio ad sexennium.

II.

Consolations of Christianity

"Whom the poets call Fortune we know to be God."

(Philipp Melanchthon, *Satires*, X, 366, c. 1520)

8.
Boethius
Five Bookes of Philosophicall Comfort
[*Consolation of Philosophy*]
Newly translated [by I. T.]
London, 1609
Sigs. E1v–E2r

In *The Consolation of Philosophy* (524), Boethius pits experience of Fortune against Philosophy's argument that a benevolent Providence actually governs human life. The paradoxical result is that the goddess of Fortune becomes something much more than the abstract idea of a deity that she had been for the Romans. Even, or particularly, in the section where Boethius' rhetorical strategy has Philosophy speak for Fortune in order to undercut her, the goddess is given a personality. The passage begins,

But I would urge thee a little with Fortune's own speeches. Wherefore consider thou, if she asketh not reason? "For what cause, O man, chargest thou mee with daily complaints? What injury have I done thee? What goods of thine have I taken from thee? Contend with mee before any judge, about the possession of riches and dignities: and if thou canst shew, that the proprietie of any of these belong to any mortall wight, I will foorthwith willingly graunt, that thos things which thou demandest, were thine.

When nature produced thee out of thy mother's wombe, I received thee naked and poore in all respects, cherished thee with my wealth, and—which maketh thee now to fall out with me—being forward to favour thee, I had most tender care for thy education, and adorned thee with the aboundance and splendour of all things, which are in my power. Now it pleaseth mee to withdraw my hand, yeeld thanks, as one that hath had the use, of that which was not his owne."

Later in the speech Philosophy has Fortune use what will become a central image in medieval art and literature: "I turn about my wheele with speed, and take a pleasure to turne things upside downe. Ascend if thou wilt, but with this condition, that thou thinkest it not an injurie to descend when the course of my sport so requireth." The wheel is the chief attribute of Fortune through much of the Middle Ages and into the early Renaissance. Typically the wheel of Fortune holds four figures, representing the conventional Latin tags, *Regno, Regnavi, Sum sine Regno, Regnabo* (I reign, I reigned, I am without reign, I shall reign).

Philosophy's subordination of Fortune to Providence is an early version of Christianity's relegation of the goddess to the sublunar realm, the world of goods rather than of the

Good, or God. Indeed, there is some attempt to attribute the power of Fortune to the Fall of Man, which created the conditions for all subsequent misfortune. The first Fall was punished by the exile of Adam and Eve from Paradise into a world of chance and change, time and death. In addition, limitations were placed on human knowledge, so that God and his powers were no longer discernible. On the one hand, this helped to explain why what humans see as the malevolence of Fortune is actually the benevolence of Providence. On the other hand, the conditions of the fallen world foster a connection among Fortune, Time, and Death. The closely related medieval *topoi* of *de casibus, contemptu mundi, ubi sunt*, and the *memento mori* Dance of Death are reflections of a similar awareness of inescapable mutability.

Opposite: Title page of Ulrich von Hutten, *Dialogi. Fortuna*, Mainz, 1520 (cat. 19).

9.
Titian
Cupid with the Wheel of Fortune
Oil on canvas
c. 1520
National Gallery of Art
Samuel H. Kress Collection (1939.1.213)

This is believed to be the only entirely monochrome painting by Titian. No completely satisfactory explanation of the imagery has been offered, but one helpful interpretation is, "Love arrests for you the precipitate wheel of fortune."[5]

10.
John Lydgate
The hystorye, sege and dystruccyon of Troye
London, 1513
Sig. E4v

Lydgate's work is a translation from the Latin of Guido delle Colonne. The woodcut shows a wheel of Fortune with its four figures. Standing behind her wheel is the goddess with wings and crown, symbols of her fleetingness and her rule. To the right is a kneeling monk, representing humility and a rejection of worldly power.

11.
Giovanni Boccaccio
A treatise excellent and compendious, shewing…the falles of…princes and princesses [*De casibus virorum illustrium*]
Adapted by John Lydgate
London, 1554
Sig. 2D1r
See Kiefer, fig. 4

This is a "many-handed" and "two-faced" Fortune. The dazzling rays streaming from her head cause the man on the right to shield his eyes. The figures on Fortune's wheel wear hats indicative of their stations

12

in life: the crowned king holding a sceptre, and behind him a cardinal, a bishop, scholars, and the hatless fallen and falling. The figure writing is Boccaccio (also wearing a scholar's hat). The left column just below the woodcut begins, "Here Bochas sittyng in his study alone, writeth a gret processe, howe fortune lyke a monstruous ymage (hauing an C [hundred] handes) apered unto hym and spake, & bochas unto her: making bytwene them both many great argumentes & reasons of fortunes chau[n]ces." Lydgate's version is based on the French by Laurent de Premierfait.

12.
Gregor Reisch
*Margarita philosophica cum
additionibus nouis*
Basel, 1517
Sig. 3i verso: "Glorior Elatus / Ad Alta Vehor / Axi Rotor / Descendo Mortificatus": "I glory in being aloft / I am carried to the heights / I am rolled beneath the wheel / I descend brought to my destruction"

In this encyclopedia of the popular science of the Renaissance, *Fortuna* holds two pots, the one on the left full, in keeping with rising fortune, the one on the right empty, for falling fortune; rather than wearing a blindfold to suggest the randomness of fortune, she either has no eyes or they are closed. While the figure at the top of the wheel waves happily, the other three cling to it in determination or desperation.

13.
A myrroure for magistrates. Wherein may be seen by example of other, with howe greuous plages vices are punished: and howe frayle and vnstable worldly prosperitie is founde, euen of those whom Fortune seemeth most highly to favour

Compiled by William Baldwin
London, 1559
Title page

Baldwin and his collaborators took the idea for their popular didactic work from Boccaccio's tales of the falls of princes. They drew on British history and legend for their moralizing stories of the tragic ends of great men. As the title indicates, however, their stories, unlike Boccaccio's, were intended to teach by presenting examples of retribution for vice. The first verse reads,

*In rufull Register of mischief and mishap,
Baldwin we beseche thee with our names
   to begin,
Whom vnfrendly Fortune did trayne vnto
   a trap,
When we thought our state most stable to
   haue bin,
So lightly leese they all which all do ween
   to wyn:
Learn by vs ye Lawyers and Iudges of the
   lande
Vncorrupt and vpryght in doome alway
   to stande.*[6]

"Base fortune, now I see, that in thy wheele
There is a point, to which when men aspire,
They tumble hedlong downe."
(Christopher Marlowe, *Edward II*, 5.6)

Especially in medieval and Renaissance images, the wheel alone sometimes represents the goddess and her powers. This iconographic synecdoche results in some inventive combinations of the wheel with other symbols that reinforce the instability and constant change that Fortune embodies. Indeed, even Fortune changes, as the wheel

gradually disappears and is replaced by other emblems of the qualities that do not change. One immediately apparent difference is that the classical Fortune, sedate and clothed, has evolved into a more active and often naked figure.

14.
Sebastian Brant
[*Narrenschiff*] *The Ship of Fooles*
Translated by Alexander Barclay
London, 1570
Page 71

In this woodcut, "Of the Mutabilitie of Fortune," copied from a German original, the wheel is sufficient to convey the idea. The ass-fools on the wheel, representing those who trust in worldly power, fall into an open grave. The Christian belief in God's ultimate control is conveyed by the hand from the clouds turning the wheel.

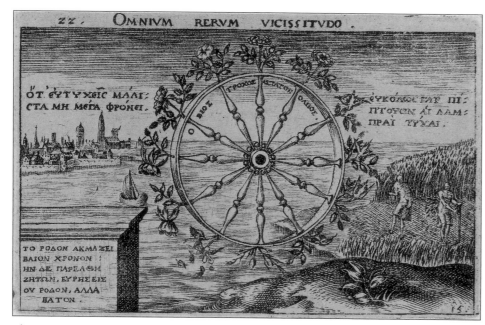

16

verse comparing the mutability of the things of nature with the constancy of Heaven.

17.
Jakob Bornitz
Emblemata ethico politica
Mainz, 1669
Book 2, page 10, no. 5: "Casus Non Casu":
"A fall not by chance"

A naked Fortune holds a sail as she falls off a wheel, which seems to be breaking because it is being pulled by a rope from the clouds; the rope, however, is broken just above Fortune's foot. The verse translates,

Nothing in the world happens by chance;
    God governs all,
Even that which you think has happened by
    Fortune's power.

18.
Allegory of Vanity
(Death Surprising a Woman)
Engraving, Italian, sixteenth century
National Gallery of Art
Rosenwald Collection (1961.17.6)
"Made Mortal They Must Die"

Human mortality is represented here by the skeleton (Death), hourglass (Time), and wheel (Fortune). Probably the female figure looks at her back, where once there were wings, symbolic of the immortal soul. One of these lies on the ground at her feet.[7]

19.
Ulrich von Hutten
Dialogi. Fortuna
Mainz, 1520
Title page
Illustrated page 14

15.
Georgette de Montenay
Liure d'armoiries en signe
Frankfurt, 1619
Page 154, XXXI: "Frangor Patientia":
"Broken by patience"
See Young, fig. 5

Although here the wheel is enough to symbolize Fortune, or rather Misfortune, note that it is the hand of God holding nettles that is the cause. A rough English version of the verse is given:

When Fortun is always with thy
So kanst thou laf merily
But if shee heids her tor a litel weyl
So thust thou, lament an cry,
Than schoulds thou, with thy remember-stil
That God sometimes [crosses] wil
Send, to thee if thou wilt by him stik
When he thy thus litel prick.

16.
Jean Jacques Boissard
Emblemes Latins
Metz, 1588
Sig. D3r: "Omnium Rerum Vicissitudo":
"The vicissitude of all things"

The constant change represented by the wheel is figured in the evanescent flowers through the stages from spring to winter, birth to death. In the background, the fields on the right are juxtaposed to the city on the left, the implication being that both are part of a natural, inevitable process. The Greek text on the left reads, "Just because you are fortunate, do not be proud"; that on the right continues, "For brilliant fortunes fall easily." The text in the box says, "For the red rose flourishes but for a short time; and if you pass by seeking it, you will find not a rose, but a bramble." On the facing page is a

This small woodcut, probably a printer's device and if so very appropriately chosen, shows a naked Fortune with all her usual accoutrements: the ball on her head, the blindfold, the cornucopia, and the sphere or globe on which she stands. Her wheel, however, is being turned by the hand of God from the right side of the picture, placing this illustration very much in the Christian tradition. The Greek text on the right reads, "Fortune helps those who think soundly"; that on the left, "It is a dreadful thing to fight with God, and Fortune." The dialogues in the book are listed below.

20.
John Florio
Firste Fruites
London, 1578
Page 47

Florio's book of simple conversations in Italian, with English translations, includes a dialogue about Fortune. One speaker tells of the great men whom Fortune has caused to fall. The second speaker replies that "man shoulde never seeke after Fortune, but altogether despise her, let her doo as she pleaseth: and all in all, put hym selfe in the handes of God." He concludes, "every one seeke Fortune, all man embrace her. None remembereth God."

21.
Le microcosme
Amsterdam, [n.d.]
Sig. F1v: "De Fortune & de sa nature": "Of Fortune and her nature"

Although not common, the image of a Fortune without feet, standing on a sphere, with sail and wings, reinforces the idea of her instability. Accompanying verses describe how the emblem represents Fortune's

DIVERS TABLEAVX

De Fortune & de sa nature.

21

inconstancy and the folly of those who trust in the goddess rather than in God.

22.
Hadrianus Junius
[*Emblemata*]
Antwerp, 1565
No. XXVI: "Fortunae instabilitas": "The instability of Fortune"

The changeable nature of Fortune is again conveyed by showing the goddess winged and footless on a sphere. The verse can be translated,

Slippery Fortune knows not how to remain in a fixed spot, is skilled in seeking new places. Hence at Smyrna the goddess was shown without feet, with feathery wings as oars.

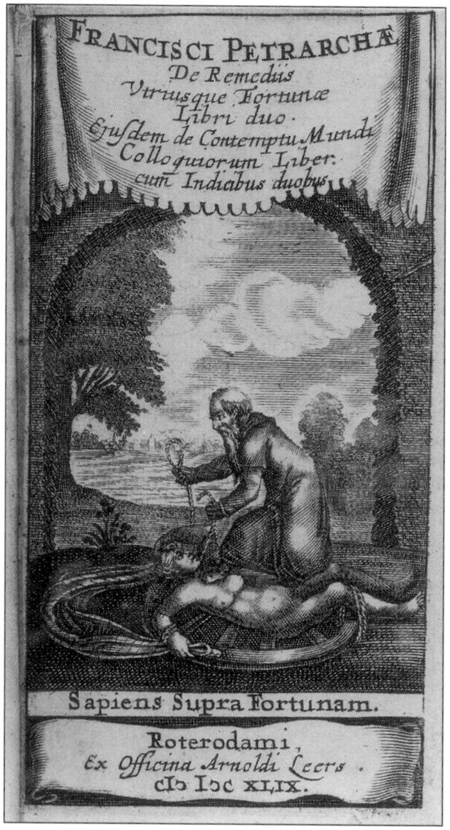

23

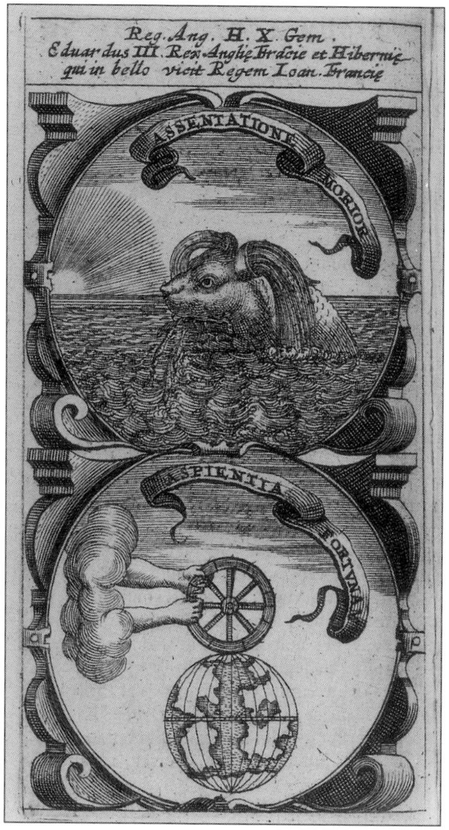

26

"Let not Fortune, which hath no name in Scripture, have any in thy divinity."
(Sir Thomas Browne, *Christian Morals*, Part i, sec. 25)

The influence of Christianity is apparent in the belief that Poverty and Wisdom are ways to avoid being trapped on Fortune's wheel and subject to her power. The irony is, however, that this approach would require a retired life, away from the temptations of the world. To lead an active life is to be subject to the control of Fortune; but an active life was the ideal for many Renaissance Humanists.

23.
Francesco Petrarca
De remediis utriusque fortunae
Rotterdam, 1649
Title page

Petrarch completed this popular work in 1366; in it a dialogue shows how to deal with not only bad fortune but good fortune as well. The image of Impoverished Wisdom tying Fortune to her wheel is probably based on the story Boccaccio tells in Book 3 of his *De Casibus* about an argument between Fortune and Poverty that ends in a fight and the result pictured here.

24.
Henry Peacham
Minerva Britanna, part 2
London, 1612
Sig. 2D3r: "Fortuna maior":
"Greater than Fortune"

This work is dedicated to Prince Henry, the son of James I, and reflects the optimism which surrounded him in 1612; he died later that year. Here the common image of Poverty tying Fortune to her wheel illustrates a Christian ideal, spelled out in the accompanying verse.

25.
Sir Thomas More
Preface to the Book of Fortune (c. 1506?)
In *Workes*, London, 1557
Sigs. C7v–C8r

In this debate-like exchange on the pros and cons of depending on Fortune, there is advice on how to avoid suffering at the hands of the goddess: "Wherefor yf [t]hou in suerte liste to stonde, / Take poverties parte & lat prowde fortune go, / Reseyue no thynge [t]hat commeth from her honde." Examples of those who trusted in Fortune and fell from her wheel, such as Alexander, Darius, and Julius Caesar, are set against others such as Socrates and Pythagoras who embraced Poverty and escaped Fortune's domination.

26.
Jacob Typot
Symbola Diuina & Humana
Arnhem, 1673
Page 286: "Aspientia Fortunam"
[i.e. Sapientia Fortunam]: "Wisdom conquers Fortune"

The combination of the earth with a wheel above, held by hands from a cloud,

illustrates the idea of the motto, that Wisdom is the way to control Fortune. A small version of this emblem can be found in the top right corner of an elaborately symbolic picture of Edward III, engraved by Renold Elstrack.

27.
Robert Southwell
Saint Peter's complaint. With other poems
London, 1595
Page 41: "Fortunes Falsehood"

The many reasons to shun Fortune are set out in this poem which implicitly contrasts a limited Fortune with the power of the Christian God. The poem ends:

No wind so changeable, no sea so wavering,
As giddy fortune in reeling vanities;
Now mad, now merciful, now fierce, now
*   favouring,*
In all things mutable but mutabilities.

28.
Guillaume de la Perrière
Le théâtre des bons engines
Paris, 1539?
No. xx

Here a blind man is led by blind Fortune with her sail. In the English edition of this work, by Thomas Coombe, the motto is "They that follow fortunes guiding, / Blindly fall with often sliding." The verse is translated,

You blinded folkes by Fortune set on hye,
Consider she is darke as well as ye,
And if your guide do want the light of eye,
You needs must fall, it can none other be.
When blind do leade the blind, they both do lye
In ditch, the Prouerbe saith, and we do see:
And those that trust to fortunes turning wheele,
Whe[n] they feare least, their fall shal
*   soonest feele.*

29.
Sir George More
A demonstration of God in his workes.
Against all such as eyther in word or
life deny there is a God
London, 1597
Pages 122–123

A printed note in the margin indicates the theme: "we make Fortune the Author of that, whereof God is the dooer, and ascribe to Chaunce, whatsoeuer is performed by the prouidence of the Almightie." There follows a vivid description of Fortune's inconstancy. On the facing page is a collection of epigrams on Fortune from classical writers.

30.
Hans Sebald Beham
Fortune
Engraving, 1541
National Gallery of Art
Rosenwald Collection (1943.3.1073)
See Kiefer, fig. 1

In this engraving, besides the wings, sphere, and wheel, there is a sheaf of wheat, another common attribute of Fortune. The man on the wheel—perhaps Beham himself?—reaches out to the goddess, as if asking to remain on the top. Fortune stands not on the sphere but on a flat surface. And the town and ship in the background seem to be experiencing good fortune. All the elements of the engraving are subtle reminders of how quickly and unexpectedly good fortune can change to bad.

31

31.
Hans Sebald Beham
Misfortune
Engraving
National Gallery of Art
Rosenwald Collection (1943.3.1074)

As the title suggests, this image is a direct contrast to *Fortune*. Here a frowning goddess is shown in motion, walking among creatures that resemble lobsters or crabs, with a devil figure behind her holding onto her skirt.

HIS FORTVNA PARENS   ILLIS INIVSTA NOVERCA EST

Fortune, the Sea, and Shakespeare's Late Plays

John H. Astington, *University of Toronto*

O diva, gratum quae regis Antium,
praesens vel imo tollere de gradu
mortale corpus vel superbos
vertere funeribus triumphos,

te pauper ambit sollicita prece
ruris colonus, te dominam aequoris
quicumque Bithyna lacessit
Carpathium pelagus carina.

(Horace, *Odes*, 1.35)[1]

As Judith Dundas points out in her essay on Spenser in this catalogue, a traditional association of Fortune's power was with that of the sea. This association had deep roots in European literature and a corresponding ancestry in the visual arts. The goddess invoked by Horace in the ode quoted above was frequently pictured on Roman coins as *Fortuna Redux*, a female figure supporting a steering oar or rudder with one hand and in the other arm holding a cornucopia, symbolizing successful venture and return, even if the "voyage" was merely a figurative one in the market. Such an image continued to be represented by Renaissance artists, in paintings, prints, and emblem books, as part of an entire range of symbolic representations of the sea and sea travel: boats, sailors, steersmen, successful voyages, and shipwrecks.

Shakespeare shows himself to have been thoroughly aware of the traditional poetic and visual representations of Fortune. In the first scene of *Timon of Athens* he introduces a Poet and a Painter who discuss symbols of Fortune's power, ominously so given what is to happen to the title character during the play. The Painter claims that pictures will always have more immediate force than verbal descriptions: "A thousand moral paintings I can show / That shall demonstrate these quick blows of Fortune's / More pregnantly than words" (1.1.90–93).[2] One of these thousands of representations was of Fortune, invariably a female figure and commonly naked, as an "arrant whore," as she is called by the Fool in *King Lear* (2.4.52): attractive, but fickle, and favoring many men in turn. Hamlet, joking with Rosencrantz and Guildenstern, knows Fortune is a "strumpet" (*Hamlet* 2.2.236), but later in the play he is saved, and Rosencrantz and Guildenstern destroyed, by a turn of fortune that happens, appropriately, on the sea. The pirates who capture Hamlet and return him, ransomed, to Denmark, had real counterparts who were a hazard to Renaissance trade and travel by water. Shylock, calculating the risks of lending money to the Venetian merchant Antonio, names them as one of the perils of an enterprise dependent on Fortune. Shakespeare

may have known that at Venice, as also at the northern port of Amsterdam, sailors and travelers might have watched a weathervane statue of Fortune, moved by the billowing sail she held, mark the changes in the wind. Shylock's shrewd judgement that "ships are but boards" (*Merchant* 1.3.22–24) is also remarkably like the contemporary Italian proverb "Chi ne legni e nei venti si confida / Alfin morte nel mar tra pesci guida"— roughly, he who trusts in the winds and in planks is heading for a watery grave. It is recorded, accompanied by a little "moral painting," or rather engraving, of a shipwreck in the sheet of *Proverbii* by the artist Niccolò Nelli (1564).[3] Alongside it appears a figure of Fortune, a naked woman holding a sail and borne aloft on the surface of the sea.

The connection between Fortune and the sea appears early in Shakespeare's work. In one of his first plays King Henry instructs the Earl of Gloucester to accompany the French ambassadors to their ships, and "Commit them to the fortune of the sea" (*The First Part of King Henry VI* 5.1.50). But in the plays written towards the end of his

---

Opposite: Fig. 1: From Theodor de Bry, *Emblemata*, Frankfurt, 1592. Courtesy of the Library of Congress.

career he gave particular prominence to the symbolic power of the sea in relation to human affairs. In *Pericles* the sea is the site of the wandering adventures of the hero, a story similar to many ancient myths and consciously referring to them, "told" by the figure of a medieval poet. Pericles endures two storms at sea: shipwrecked after the first, he finds his wife Thaisa; during the second he appears to lose her, and her supposedly dead body is cast adrift in a floating coffin. Discovery and loss through the agency of the sea form a theme already explored by Shakespeare in the comedy *Twelfth Night*; in that play the bereavement caused by ship-wreck is finally repaired, and as Viola had hoped, "Tempests are kind and salt waves fresh in love" (3.4.384). While characters endure them, however, tempests do not appear to be kind. Beyond any human control and unresponsive to human appeals, as King Lear discovers, they might stand for the power of forces indifferent to the fate of men and women. The storm is an emblem of the force of destructive accident. In *Pericles* such accidents may indeed be directed by a Fortune which is actively malevolent; yet her force may be withstood by human determination and the help of favorable gods. Gower sums up the progress of the play towards its end:

In Antiochus and his daughter you have heard
Of monstrous lust the due and just reward.
In Pericles, his queen and daughter, seen,
Although assail'd with fortune fierce and keen,
Virtue [preserv'd] from fell destruction's blast,
Led on by heaven, and crown'd with joy at last.
                                            (5.3.85–90)

The adventures of *Cymbeline* do not have a great deal to do with the sea, but the diffi-culties in which the characters are enmeshed bring to the mind of one of them the perils of a sea journey. The loyal servant Pisanio, like Viola in *Twelfth Night* hoping for a fortunate outcome to a perplexing situation, reflects that "Fortune brings in some boats that are not steer'd" (4.3.46). The steering of boats—the direction of one's course through life—normally forms an important part of Shakespeare's moral view; here he recognizes the occasional importance of benign luck in arriving at one's destination. Actual sea journeys return to the stage in *The Winter's Tale*. The play is famously divided into two halves, the second introduced by "Time, the Chorus," who announces that he is going to slide us over sixteen years before the dramatic fiction begins again. Immediately before his appearance, Antigonus lands from the ship which has brought him to the fictitious coast of Bohemia to expose the infant Perdita to Fortune. As he lays the baby down, "The storm begins" (3.3.49), and Fortune shows her power: the baby is saved by the Shepherd, Antigonus is chased and killed by a bear, and the ship is wrecked in the storm and her crew drowned. And to escape the anger of Polixenes it is to the sea again that the sixteen-year-old Perdita commits herself with her lover, Florizel; "Fortune speed us!" he cries, as they are about to embark (4.4.667). The second voyage is to undo the damage of the first, and hence is prosperous.

Shakespeare gave to *The Tempest* a title which recognized a persistent dramatic image of his entire work, and to the power of the sea in the play he gave an entire range of associations, both destructive and restorative, like the strange "sea change" of which Ariel sings to Ferdinand in the second scene. The play begins with a stage image that to Renaissance eyes immediately would have invoked the destructive power of Fortune. The foundering or sinking ship was the victim of the goddess immemorially associated with the sea. So in the image from De Bry's *Emblemata* (Frankfurt, 1592), Fortune stands centrally on a ball floating on the waves, with a sail billowing out behind her; her right hand extends blessings to the voyagers on one side of the picture, while to her left a wrecked ship sinks and an unfortunate man drowns (fig. 1). Prospero speaks overtly only once of "bountiful Fortune" (1.2.178–84), yet *The Tempest* is pervaded with references to the mythology and iconography of Fortune. Thus the ending of the play restores the apparently wrecked ship, and the travelers resume their journey, accompanied by some new colleagues and the promise of "calm seas, auspicious gales, / And sail so expeditious, that shall catch / Your royal fleet far off" (5.1.315–17). Here we might say that Prospero seems to speak with the voice of Fortune, but the promised seascape is that of the left half of the De Bry emblem ("HIS FORTVNA PARENS"— to these people Fortune is a kind mother), the play having begun in the right half.

The moral of the sailing vessel at the mercy of bad weather might be read as the limited power of human ingenuity in the face either of pagan chance or of God's will at work through the agency of nature. This general theme was susceptible to various shades of coloring. The wise and experienced steersman or captain might save the ship from adverse weather; the sail of bad Fortune, blowing one into the rocks, might be counteracted by the rudder of skill. The central question of the first scene of *The Tempest* is the correct navigation of the endangered ship; noisy discord accompanies the gale and high waves as the arrogant courtiers "mar" the "labor" of those who should be in control. The emblematic point of the "bawling" and aimless running about in this scene would have been immediately grasped by its first audiences. The ship was

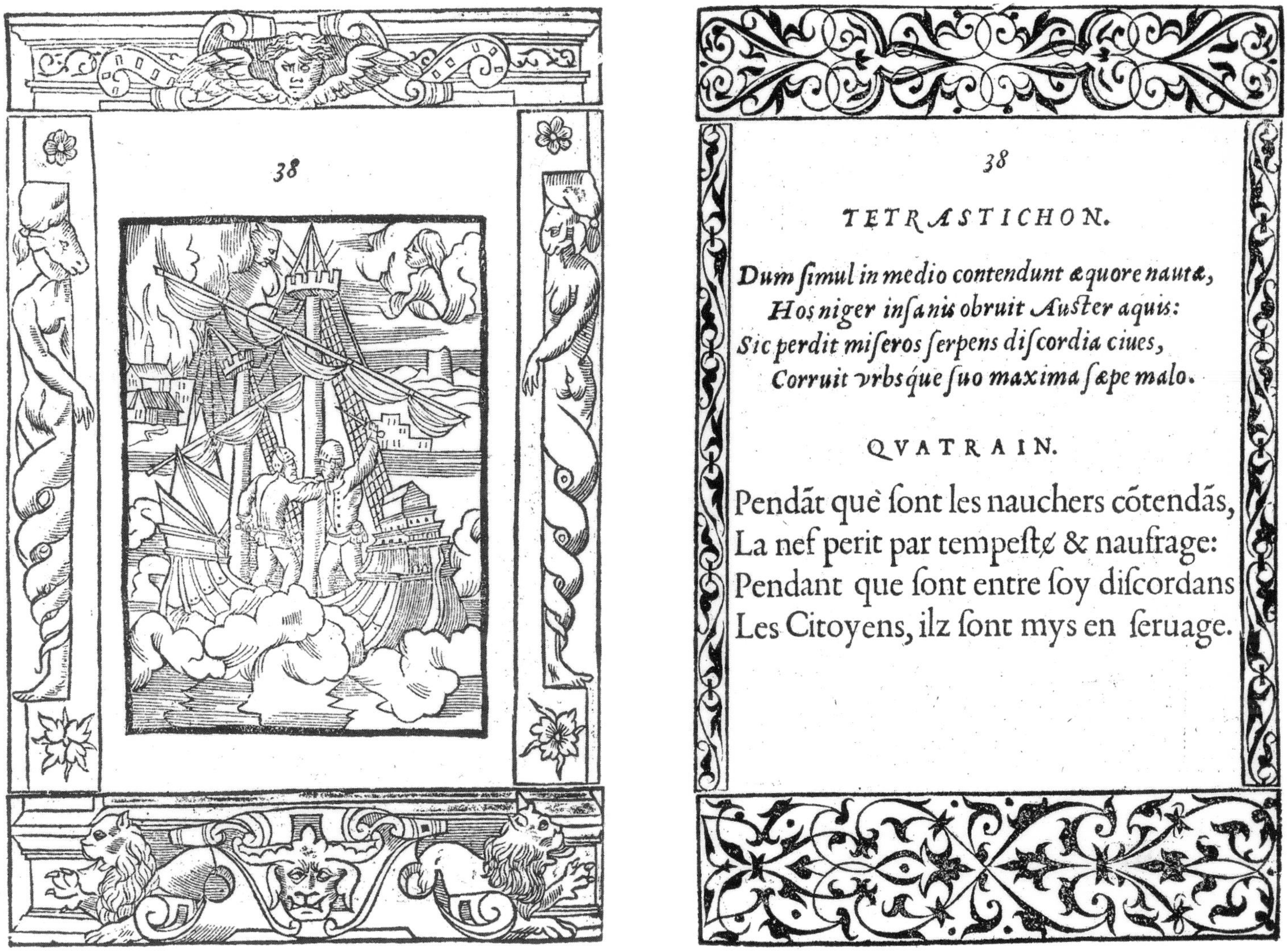
38

TETRASTICHON.

Dum ſimul in medio contendunt æquore nautæ,
Hos niger inſanis obruit Auſter aquis:
Sic perdit miſeros ſerpens diſcordia ciues,
Corruit vrbsque ſuo maxima ſæpe malo.

QVATRAIN.

Pendāt que ſont les nauchers cōtendās,
La nef perit par tempeſte & naufrage:
Pendant que ſont entre ſoy diſcordans
Les Citoyens, ilz ſont mys en ſeruage.

Fig. 2: From Guillaume de la Perrière, *La Morosophie*, Lyons, 1553.

a principal symbol of human community and shared enterprise: unless its occupants worked together to the same end it was at risk of wreckage. Symbolic ships were particularly popular in literature and woodcuts at the beginning of the sixteenth century, with Brant's *Ship of Fools* standing as the most famous antitype of communal order and discipline.[4]

As the individual might arm himself against Fortune's buffets, then so might the community: a divided crew put the ship in danger. Such is the point of Emblem 38 from Guillaume de la Perrière's *La Morosophie* (1553; fig. 2). Two sailors fight as their ship founders in rough seas; in the background, as in the De Bry picture, is a city in flames, an application of the metaphor of civic disaster. The accompanying quatrain reads "Pendant que sont les nauchers contendans, / La nef perist par tempeste & naufrage: /

Pendant que sont entre soy discordans / Les Cytoyens, ilz sont mys en seruage" (While the sailors struggle the ship runs aground in the storm; so civil strife will lead to the bondage of everyone). Not only should the ship's complement work together to one end, however, but the master of the ship should be in firm control, directing the course. This general analogy of skill, authority and responsibility, from ship's master to the prince, casts its shadow over the entire length of *The Tempest*. An image from Bocchi's *Symbolicae Quaestiones* (1574), showing a ship with a crew at work, might be taken as an example of this commonplace (fig. 3). The accompanying Latin verses survey the lively physical activity of the young sailors, but point out that their labor is directed by the experienced old man at the helm. "In puppi residens clauum tenet ille quietus, / At non quae iuuenem robora, strenuuitas, / Quin multo maiora facit, melioraque solus / Ipse suo praestans omnibus ingenio, / res magnae haud valido, aut veloci corpore fiunt, / Verum animi sensu, consilio, imperio." The last two lines might be rendered in English as "Great things are not done by physical power or agility, / But rather by mental insight, wisdom, and authority." The exercise of such skill in the face of Fortune's power is a further variation on the general maritime analogy.

After the breaking ship of the first scene of *The Tempest*, the second vessel we encounter, in Prospero's story, is the "rotten carcass of a butt," the derelict boat in which Prospero and the infant Miranda were cast adrift twelve years since. The stage designer Maria Bjornson emphasized the connection between the two vessels in the eyes of a modern audience by placing the wrecked ribs of a ship on the set throughout: the opening shipwreck was played within what

CLVIII   LIB. III.

RES CONSILII OPE, HAVD VIRIBVS MAGNAS GERI.

Symb. LXXIIII.

Fig. 3: From Achille Bocchi, *Symbolicae Quaestiones*, Bologna, 1574 (first published 1555).

became the ghost of the earlier boat (Royal Shakespeare Company, Stratford, 1982). Deprived of a sail and rigging (no rudder is mentioned) the lifeboat is more than usually dependent on Fortune. The waves and winds in Prospero's description are sympathetic to human suffering, however, and while chance may save as many as it destroys, the arrival at the island seems to Prospero to be thanks to the agency of "Providence divine," not Fortune. But Providence also has a human agent in the boat, an inspiring principle in the shape of Prospero's daughter.

> *O a cherubin*
> *Thou wast that did preserve me. Thou*
>   *didst smile*
> *Infused with a fortitude from heaven,*
> *When I have decked the sea with drops*
>   *full salt,*
> *Under my burthen groan'd, which rais'd in me*
> *An undergoing stomach, to bear up*
> *Against what should ensue.*
>   (1.2.152–58)

The symbolic female figure in a boat recurs in many forms in emblematic language of the period. Commonly the figure is a naked Fortuna with a sail, standing in the place of a mast, and in that form serving as another symbol of the uncertainty and danger of the sea. A carving at the Palazzo Rucellai in Florence preserves such a Fortuna used as a coat of arms,[5] and in an emblem from Boissard's *Emblematum Liber* (Metz, 1595) the Fortune boat is used in direct opposition to symbols of human wisdom and knowledge (cat. 87, fig. 4). Wisdom sits with her back turned to the sea, surrounded, like Prospero, with books, and other tools of human learning; she shuns the uncertainty of the voyage of Fortune sailing in search of riches.

But figures of moral guidance, indeed of "fortitude from heaven," could be placed in

Fig. 4: From Jean Jacques Boissard, *Emblemes*, Metz, 1595 (cat. 87).

Fortune's boat. Such is the motif of a series of woodblock printers' marks from the presses of Domenico and Pietro de' Franceschi, publishers of Palladio's *I Quattro Libri dell' Architettura* at Venice in 1570. That famous folio bears a Fortune boat at the lower center of the title page. A variant mark (cat. 59, fig. 5) also shows Fortune's boat, with the goddess providing the motive power, standing in the prow, approaching a harbor. In the stern sits a female figure wearing a crown and holding a sceptre; she steers the boat by its rudder, and the gunwale bears her title, "REGINA VIRTUS." Virtue directs the opportunities that Fortune offers; the motto, printed on either side of the block, might remind us of the Latinate name of the chief character in *The Tempest*: "DVCIBVS HIS / PROSPERA QVAEQVE" (Led by these everyone

[will find] prosperity).

That the visual motif had found its way to the British Isles by the early seventeenth century is proved by its presence among the ceiling paintings at Pinkie House, just outside Edinburgh, made for Alexander Seton in 1613. There the figure at the helm is male, representing the legendary steersman of the Argonauts, Tiphys, but the moral emblem painted over the picture is the same: "Sit Virtus Tiphys" (Let Tiphys be Virtue)— only the virtuous can successfully steer the boat of Fortune.[6] Having been presented by "bountiful Fortune" with the opportunity of righting the wrongs done to him, Prospero must steer the course of his action with skill, and it is perhaps significant, given the motif I have just described, that at a crucial juncture he chooses virtue over vengeance.

Fig. 5: Woodcut printer's mark of Domenico and Pietro de' Franceschi, in Orazio Toscanella, *Discorsi cinque*, Venice, 1575 (cat. 59).

Steering the boat blown by potentially malevolent forces was also an emblem of specifically Christian ethics, and the theme seems to have been particularly popular in Germany in the mid-sixteenth century. A bronze plaque and a metal shield both show a lightly draped standing female figure in a small boat. She has long hair, blown with the wind that has ripped the sail behind her, and she at first appears to be in the line of the maritime Fortuna, but she wields a long steering oar and is not allowing the boat to drift; she is rather a version of *Fortitudo*.[7] An elaborate working out of this iconographic tradition may be seen in a carved limewood relief of 1534 by Peter Dell the Elder (1495–1552), preserved in the Germanisches National-museum in Nuremberg.[8] Like the *Regina Virtus*, the steerswoman in this carving is fully dressed, and seated; she is directing her boat towards the heavenly haven, on the right, where Christ casts out a line to the approaching vessel. The labels tell us that the hull of the boat is flesh and blood, the sail

love and patience, and the rudder the Christian life. A shield at the foot of the mast represents faith, and in the prow is the compass of God's word. Rather than Fortuna, the adverse forces assailing the vessel are sea monsters representing the world, death, and the devil, but the composition is recognizably a variation on the theme of the moral voyage. Once again, it is clear that such allegorizing was known in England, and it continued well into the seventeenth century. In 1636 there appeared a broadside entitled *The State of a Christian Lively Set Forth by an Allegorie of a Shippe under Sayle* (STC 26112.7). It plays many variations on the relationships between the individual and the parts of a ship; of particular interest in relation to the opening of *The Tempest* is the following passage: "My *Noble Passengers* are Ioy in the holy Ghost & the peace of Conscience, whose *retinue* are divine graces; my *ignoble* or rather *mutinous* passengers are worldly cogitations and vaine delights, which are more than a good many; besides some that are *arrant theeves* and *traytors*, namely pride, envie, prejudice; but all these ile bid farewell when I come to my journeis end, though I would but cannot before."

Guided by Fortune, "immortal Providence," and Prospero's direction of events, all the participants in *The Tempest* bring their boats to harbor:

> in one voyage
> *Did Claribel her husband find at Tunis,*
> *And Ferdinand, her brother, found a wife*
> *Where he himself was lost; Prospero, his dukedom*
> *In a poor isle; and all of us, ourselves,*
> *When no man was his own.*
>
> (5.1.208–13)

If the ship is frequently a symbol of community, then—Prospero has not paid enough attention to the helm of state, and must regain it from those who have

mutinied against him—each individual is also directing his or her course over the sea of life. The union of lovers, or of man and wife, is also subject to the power of Fortune, and variations on the visual representations of Fortune's power could be directed specifically to the course of love. In a painting in a German *stammbuch*, or *album amicorum*, from 1641 a pair of lovers on the left is matched with a particularly exuberant Fortuna on the right. They have successfully subdued blind Amor (the "waspish-headed son" of Venus who is excluded from the ceremonies marking the marriage contract of Miranda and Ferdinand), but if they embark on the sea of marriage—a progress suggested by the spring emerging from the cliff in the background to their left (itself an old image of female sexuality) and flowing out into the wide sea on which Fortuna rides—they must reckon with being able to withstand the vicissitudes of their journey together.

Fortuna's boat as an image of love occurs very early in iconographic history: the anonymous print "The Ship of Fortune" was made in Florence in the 1460s.[9] It plays the remarkable variation of turning the central youthful nude figure holding the sail into a male; a clothed young woman sits in the stern, suggesting it is she who controls the course of the ship (although she does not grasp a tiller or steering oar). Winds blow on the boat from various points of the compass, and from both above and below; above on the right hovers a Cupid holding an arrow. The complete legend in undamaged versions of the print translates as "I allow myself to be carried by Fortune, hoping in the end to have good luck." The speaker might be either figure in the boat, although logically it should be the woman: she is not steering since she has abandoned herself to erotic Fortune.

The naked figure of Fortune, in the boat or riding on the sea, is primarily erotic, attracting desire while suggesting the destructive dangers of blind passion. The seaborne goddess (far more usually than the naked male) has associations cognate with the great deity of love, Venus: De Bry's *Fortuna* (see fig. 1) rides on a ball which is supported in turn on a scallop shell. Botticelli's famous Venus rides to land on precisely this symbol. We might say, then, that one way of reading the ship emblems of Fortuna is that they indicate the need to direct passion by reason, precisely as Prospero wants the young lovers in *The Tempest* to do (4.1.1–56). Unpredictable sexual power requires the guidance of a skilled, thoughtful steersman / woman.

The motif of marriage as a voyage is interestingly picked up in an English source published in 1607, a few years before *The Tempest*. The words of *The Merchant Royall* were spoken at court, in the presence of King James and his chief courtiers, as a sermon preached by Dr. Robert Wilkinson, minister of St. Olave's in Southwark. The occasion was the marriage of Lord Hay to Honora Denny, on Twelfth Night, 6 January 1607; in the evening Thomas Campion's masque in honor of the occasion was presented in the Hall. Wilkinson's text was Proverbs, 31.14: "Shee is like a Marchants Shippe, shee bringeth her food from a farre." Wilkinson's development of this rather unpromising start is worth quoting at some length, since his opening theme, although he does not give it the title, is Fortune.

O what time might a man aske to set downe all the miseries of this life! the feare, the care, the anguish that daily accompanieth the body and soule of man; the labours & sorrowes certaine, the casualties uncertaine, the

contentions and unquietnesse of them that live among us, the sharpe assaultes and oppositions of them that hate us, but chi[e]fly the unfaithfulnesse and treacherie of them that seeme to love us: against these stormes to save men from drowning did God ordaine the woman, as a shippe upon the sea, that as Noah *made an Arke, and by that Arke escaped the floude, so man by marrying with the woman might passe through all the labors of this life, unto which doubtlesse God had respect when he said,* It is not good for man to bee alone, let us make a helpe meete for him: *as much as to say, a ship to save him, therefore hee which hath no wife may seeme to be like Ionas in the sea, left in the midst of a miserable worlde to sinke or swim, or shift for himselfe; but then comes a wife like a ship and wafts him home.*[10]

The ship which is to waft everyone home at the end of *The Tempest*, then, contains within its multiple symbolism the motif of the happy and successful marriage, in which both partners guide each other "Out of this fearful country" (5.1.106), the realm which Wilkinson describes as being governed only by the uncertainties of Fortune.

Notes

1. *O goddess ruling over favoured Antium,*
    With power to raise our perishable bodies
    From low degree or turn
    The pomp of triumph into funeral,

    Thee the poor farmer with his worried prayer
    Propitiates; thee, mistress of the ocean,
    Whoever dares the seas
    Round Crete in a Bithynian-timbered boat

    Entreats

    The Odes of Horace, trans. James Michie (London, 1964), 80–83.

2. All quotations from *The Riverside Shakespeare*, ed G. Blakemore Evans, 2nd ed. (Boston, 1997).

3. See Sarah F. Matthews Grieco, "Pedagogical Prints: Moralizing Broadsheets and Wayward Women in Counter Reformation Italy," *Picturing Women in Renaissance and Baroque Italy*, ed. Geraldine A. Johnson and Sarah F. Matthews Grieco (Cambridge, 1997), 61–87: 77–86.

4. See R. Scribner, *For the Sake of Simple Folk* (Cambridge, 1981), 106–15.

5. See Frederick Kiefer, *Fortune and Elizabethan Tragedy* (San Marino, 1983), 194–98.

6. See Michael Bath, "Alexander Seton's Painted Gallery," *Albion's Classicism*, ed. Lucy Gent (New Haven, 1995), 79–108. The Tiphys painting is illustrated as Fig. 58.

7. For an illustration and discussion of the shield, which is dated 1543, see G. F. Laking, *A Record of European Armour and Arms*, 5 vols. (London, 1920–1922); vol. 4, 239–42. The oar is labeled "forteza" and the boat "caro" (flesh); the sea bears the legend "vortuna." In the prow are a shield and an urn: "Fides" and "gracia dei."

8. See Jeffrey Chipps Smith, *German Sculpture of the Later Renaissance c. 1520–1580* (Princeton, 1994), 66–68.

9. See *The Illustrated Bartsch*, vol. 24, *The Early Italian Masters*, Commentary Part 2, ed. Mark J. Zucker (New York, 1994), 131–32.

10. Robert Wilkinson, *The Merchant Royall* (London, 1607, STC 25657), 6. The title page of the quarto bears a woodcut illustration of a ship.

III.

Fortune, Occasion, Nemesis

"If a man look sharply and attentively, he shall see Fortune;
for though she is blind, she is not invisible."

(Sir Francis Bacon, "Of Fortune," *Essays*, 1612)

Despite the insistence of Christianity and, no doubt, widespread belief in the idea of an unknowable Providence, the everyday experience of Fortune's power was unchanged. Perhaps as a direct consequence, Fortune gradually took on the attributes of two other goddesses, Occasion and Nemesis. Even here she seems to dominate. Aside from this irony, however, the real significance of this change in the iconography of Fortune is that it implies that men can control her by being ready to take advantage of opportunity, and by not reaching too high. This conflation quite explicitly reflects the attempt of Christian Humanism to resolve the battle between freedom and necessity by showing how the individual who is in control of himself can control his Fortune.[8]

A related idea that gains force during the Renaissance is that of Fortune as female. "*Fortuna*" is gendered feminine in Latin—as a word, not as a concept; so too is *Superbia* (Pride), but so also are *Sapientia* (Wisdom), *Patientia* (Patience), *Castitas* (Chastity), and *Justitia* (Justice) among others. Since, however, women were considered to have inherited the qualities attributed to Eve— disobedience, stubbornness, changeability— it is not surprising that the idea of Fortune as a woman develops as it does in both verbal and visual representations of her during this

period. Indeed, this conception of Fortune does not really evolve until the Christian era, possibly in part as a way of undercutting the goddess as a powerful figure to be worshipped and propitiated, but also because Fortune shares the negative qualities of Eve with other female figures imagined as temptations from the Good, such as Pride, the Whore of Babylon, Helen of Troy, and Venus. When Fortune, who is usually clothed and rather matronly in Roman and medieval representations, is gradually conflated in the emblem books of the Renaissance with Occasion, who is usually naked, a more seductive temptress is the result.

The popular emblem book genre, of which there are many examples in this exhibition, began with the book of epigrams, or *emblemata*, as he called them, of Andrea Alciato, which in their original form were without pictures—ironically, given what the word has come to mean; and although this work continues to be referred to under his name (usually spelled Alciati), he did not produce any of the pictures added in 1531 to illustrate his words. The influence of these combinations of motto, picture, and verse was enormous; there were over two hundred editions in the sixteenth and seventeenth centuries, with gradually more sophisticated pictures that help to chart the evolution of

the genre.[9] Although Alciato had written his verses for private circulation among his friends, and his purpose was to entertain and amuse, as the emblem book developed it came to be seen as an appealing way to teach and moralize. Not surprisingly, the Humanists had a particular fondness for emblems, with their personifications and visual representations of abstract concepts such as virtues and vices. The classical writers rediscovered by the Humanists were the source of many ideas allegorized in emblems, something to which the emblematists proudly called attention. After the publication of the first illustrated Alciato collection, the genre was quickly established on the continent, but it did not move to England until well into the reign of Queen Elizabeth. And until the end of the seventeenth century, when the form largely disappeared, the continental emblem books were always more original, varied, and numerous than their English counterparts.

Opposite: From *Stirpium, insignium nobilitatis*, Basel, 1602? (cat. 43).

"He that will not when he may,
When he would he shall have nay."
(John Heywood, *Proverbs*, Part i, ch. 3, 1546)

On her own, Occasion or Opportunity is a goddess linked to Time, as is evident in the conventional image of a figure with a head which has a forelock in the front but is bald in the back. Those who would "seize the occasion" must be able to see it coming and grab it before it passes, or there is nothing to grab. Occasion is always naked, perhaps to suggest that she should be easy to recognize. These characteristics imply that Opportunity can be controlled by those who are smart enough and quick enough.

32.
Andrea Alciato
Emblematum libellus
Paris, 1534
Page 20

This is one of the early versions of Occasion, with bald head and forelock, winged feet, and a razor. The verse translates,

This image is the work of Lysippus, whose home was Sicyon.–Who are you?–I am the moment of seized opportunity that governs all.–Why do you stand on points?–I am always whirling about.–Why do you have winged sandals on your feet?–The fickle breeze bears me in all directions.–Tell us, what is the reason for the sharp razor in your right hand?–This sign indicates that I am keener than any cutting edge.– Why is there a lock of hair on your brow?–So that I may be seized as I run towards you.–But come, tell us now, why ever is the back of your head bald?–So that if any person once lets me depart on my winged feet, I may not thereafter be caught by having my hair seized. It was for your sake, stranger, that the craftsman produced me with such art, and, so that I should warn all, it is an open portico that holds me.[10]

32

33.
Andrea Alciato
Emblemata
Lyons, 1591
Page 449

The better known Alciato-inspired image of Occasion in this edition appears later in a modified version in Whitney's collection of emblems. The image is also reworked by Crispijn van de Passe in emblem books by Rollenhagen and Wither.

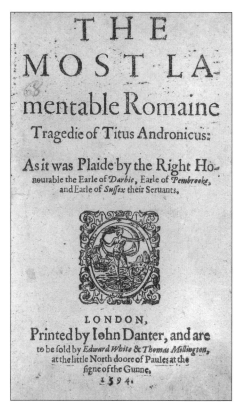

34

34.
William Shakespeare
The most lamentable Romaine Tragedie of Titus Andronicus
Unique copy of Quarto 1
London, 1594
Title page printer's device of John Danter

The popularity of this version of Occasion or Opportunity is suggested by its use as a printer's device. Note that the image has evolved so that the cloth Fortune holds now surrounds her upper half. Also, here there are two ships in the background, one of which is sinking, suggesting not so much lost opportunity as good and bad Fortune on the ever-changing sea.

35

36

35.
Gabriel Rollenhagen
Nucleus emblematum selectissimorum
Cologne, 1611
Book 1, no. 4: "Ne Tenear":
"May I not be held"

Crispijn van de Passe's version of this
emblem of Occasion was adapted from that
in Alciato. Here, as in some other emblem
books, the naked female body has been
"censored" with a swipe of ink by a reader.

36.
Achille Bocchi
Symbolicarum quaestionum
Bologna, 1555
Book 3, no. LXIX: "Occasionem Qui Sapis
Ne Amiseris": "You who are wise, do not let
chance slip by"

In this engraving by Bonasone, Occasion has
wings on her heels and a forelock and is
poised precariously on the wheel of Fortune.
The accompanying Latin verse urges the
reader to "Know the Time."

37.
Otto van Veen
Les emblemes de l'amour humain
Brussels, 1668
Sig. Y4r: "Undecumque Occasio Promta":
"Whensoever Opportunity offers"

Cupid pulls the forelock of Occasion as she
bows to him, offering a cornucopia filled
with fruit and flowers. On the left, ivy winds
itself around a root, branch, and tree. The
English version of the verse, titled "Love
useth manie meanes" is,

The ivie ought can fynd his weaknes to supporte,
So doth the lover seek his fastning hold to take,
Of each occasion meet, advantage for to make,
For ought must overslip that may his good
   importe.

38.
Jan David
Occasio arrepta, neglecta
Antwerp, 1605
Title page

Theodore Galle engraved this elaborate title page illustrating the idea of Occasion in various contexts. The top circle shows "Occasio Rei": an iron being struck while the anvil is hot. On the left is "Occasio Temporis": an army drives off the enemy before the sun has set; on the right, "Occasio Locis": an army emerging from a castle to drive off besiegers. In the center panel on the left, a soldier grasps Occasion by the forelock; on the right, Occasion slips away unnoticed while a man sleeps at the tiller. Just below, on the left, Judith kills the sleeping Holofernes; on the right are what appear to be soldiers wasting time gambling and carousing. At the bottom on the left, a woman sitting between a chest and a barrel under a row of crowns holds a cornucopia; on the right a dejected man with chains, handcuffs, and a halter above him sits before the fires of hell. This work is overtly Christian, emphasizing the human ability to control Fortune by seizing Opportunity. The book concludes with a Latin play about Occasion.[11]

39.
Cornelis Schut
Neptune on the Sea and Fortune on a Sphere held by Occasio
Etching
National Gallery of Art
Ailsa Mellon Bruce Fund (1972.28.94)
See Dundas, fig. 1

Here the association of both Fortune and Occasion with the sea is represented by the presence of Neptune, perhaps helping the

cooperative union of the two goddesses, who ride in a boat that seems to have a dolphin, another of Fortune's companions, under it.

"Nemesis is that recoil of Nature, not to be guarded against, which ever surprises the most wary transgressor."
(Ralph Waldo Emerson, *Journals*, 1864)

The Renaissance concept of Nemesis is not what we might expect. Rather than retribution, Nemesis and her accoutrements usually symbolize moderation and the self-discipline necessary to achieve it. When punishment is a factor, it is the idea of justice that dominates. This Nemesis represents the restraint of pride and overreaching ambition, as well as necessity. From antiquity onwards, depictions of Nemesis frequently show her holding some sort of vessel, usually a bowl or urn, suggestive of reward. Thus both the good and the bad, give and take, can be aspects of this goddess. For whatever reason, Nemesis is often pictured from the side, striding through a landscape.

40.
Jean Baudoin
Recueil d'emblemes divers
Paris, 1638–1639
Vol. 1, page 484: "Qu'il ne faut iamais offenser personne, ny de fait, ny de parole"

Wither translates this motto, "Doe not the golden Meane exceed, / In Word, in Passion, nor in Deed." Nemesis is shown with her usual accoutrements: a halter or bridle signifying the need for self-control, and a cubit-rule or square representing the rule of law.

41.
[Nathaniel Crouch]
Choice Emblems, Divine and Moral
London, 1732
No. XI: "Serva Modum": "Keep the Mean"

Again, Nemesis keeps one on the straight and narrow path of moderation—therefore neither a victim of temptation, nor subject to the ups and downs of Fortune.

42.
Geoffrey Whitney
A choice of emblemes, and other deuises
Leiden, 1586
Page 19

As the title suggests, virtually all the emblems in this famous book are from earlier continental collections—this one from Alciato. The interpretive verse below the picture does not accord with the usual idea of Nemesis, but it is one that Whitney inherited. The "wicked imps" referred to in the verse are represented by footsteps on the ground, which Nemesis follows.

43.
Stirpium, insignium nobilitatis
Basel, 1602?
Page 1: "Homo vanitatis et fortuna ludibrium": "Man, and Fortune, a mockery of his vanity"
Illustrated page 30.

The conflation of Nemesis and Occasion with Fortune is apparent in this engraving by Crispijn van de Passe which shows Fortune on a sphere, naked except for a veil, tossing away material goods but also with the bridle associated with Nemesis and the forelock of Occasion. She stands at the entrance to "The gate of human life" between

42

Heraclitus on the left and Democritus on the right. The writing on the arch is translated above; the verse reads,

What should I do? Heraclitus, should I weep with you through my laughter?
For who withholds a smile seeing everything filled with Folly?
Or whether with Democritus one should blame the affairs of men,
Who seeing such a mixture of woe can withhold tears?

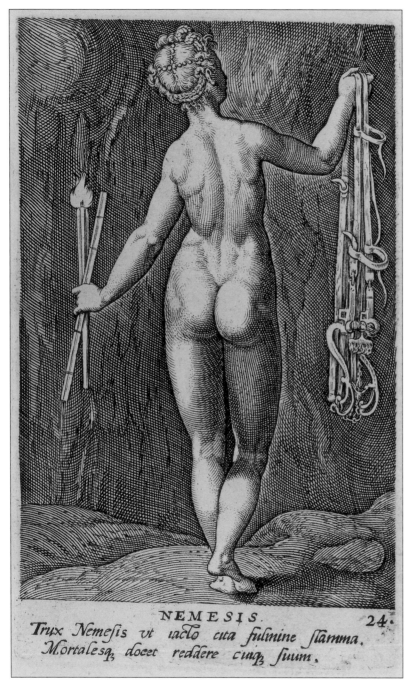

NEMESIS.   24.

Trux Nemesis vt iacto cita fulmine flamma.
Mortalesq, docet reddere cinq, suum.

44

22,

NEMESIS, *or the Viciſſitude*
of things.

NEmeſis is ſaid to be a Goddeſſe
venerable vnto all , but to bee
feared of none but potentates and
fortunes fauorites. She is thought
to be the Daughter of *Oceanus* and
Nox. Shee is purtrayed with
wings on her ſhoulders, and on her
head a Coronet;bearing in her right
hand a iauelin of Aſh , and in her
left a Pitcher with the ſimilitudes of
Æthiopians engrauen on it : and
laſtly ſhee is deſcribed ſitting on a
Hart.

The Parable may bee thus vn-
folded. Her name *Nemeſis* doth
plainly ſignifie Reuenge or Retribution,her office and adminiſtration
being(like a Tribune of the people)
to hinder the conſtant & perpetuall
felicity of happy men , and to inter-
poſe her word,*veto,*I forbid the con-
tinuance of it, that is , not onely to
                                    E 2   chaſtice

45

44.
Philippe Galle
De Deis Gentium Imagines
Antwerp, 1581
No. 24: "Trux Nemesis ut iacto cua fulmine
flamma. Mortalesq[ue], docet reddere
cinq[ue], suum": "Savage is Nemesis when
the bolt of flame is cast. She teaches mortals
to give back what is due"

This unusual emblem by de Bry shows a
naked Nemesis from the back; she holds the
measure and bridle, as well as a torch.

45.
Francis Bacon
The wisedome of the ancients
Translated by Sir Arthur Gorges
London, 1619
Sig. E2r

Bacon's discussion of one version of the classical Nemesis details her parentage, accoutrements, and characteristics in order to emphasize her retributive role.

46.
Albrecht Dürer
Nemesis (The Great Fortune)
Engraving, c. 1501/1502
National Gallery of Art
The Gift of R. Horace Gallatin (1949.1.21)

In Dürer's depiction, Nemesis carries her traditional goblet and bridle; she also wears wings and stands on a sphere, as Fortune often does. Her size, physique, and position high above a landscape all convey her power. Not surprisingly, the work has two titles.[12]

"He that waits upon fortune is never sure of a dinner."
(Benjamin Franklin, *Poor Richard's Almanac*, 1734)

The changeability of Fortune's image, especially as a consequence of artists' inclination to bestow on her the qualities and attributes of Occasion and Nemesis, can be traced in the many different representations of the goddess. Although no single image evolves as the dominant one, the concept of Fortune gradually becomes more fixed, less varied, and more inclusive. In Italian *fortuna* can mean "tempest" or "storm," and certainly

46

this is a common aspect of depictions of Fortune, particularly in combination with the sea and ships, where the wind of Fortune can be beneficial or destructive, sometimes amenable to human control, and sometimes not. Fortune is shown most often in an open space, implying that she cannot be contained. Renaissance iconography often shows the goddess naked, which is seen as a sign of purity by some, of seductiveness by others. Her nakedness also suggests that it should be easy to see what she represents. The sail and sphere, always associated with Fortune, are regularly accompanied by some combination of wings, blindfold, forelock, cornucopia, crown, sceptre, dolphin, and still sometimes the wheel.

47.
William Shakespeare
The most excellent and lamentable tragedie, of Romeo and Juliet
London, 1599
Sigs. H3v–H4r

In the second quarto of *Romeo and Juliet*, just after Romeo has climbed down from Juliet's balcony to flee to Mantua, Juliet invokes the goddess and gives the notion of "fickle Fortune" an optimistic turn:

O Fortune, Fortune, all men call thee fickle,
If thou art fickle, what dost thou with him
That is renownd for faith? be fickle Fortune:
For then I hope thou wilt not keepe him long,
But send him backe.

49

48.
Francis Bacon
Historia regni Henrici septimi
Amsterdam, 1662
Title page

Fortune, with a forelock and with wings on her back, stands on a sphere and holds out a covered goblet and bridle in one hand. The wheel she turns, with its symbols of high to low status, is being stopped, as is the sphere on which she stands, by two men on solid ground who represent wisdom. On her other side, two flatterers share the goddess's platform and caress her. The water and ships in the background represent the vicissitudes of fortune.

49.
Vincenzo Cartari
Le imagini de i dei de gli antichi
Venice, 1571
Page [465]

Each of these images, ostensibly of Nemesis, is based on a different mythological description. On the left, the winged goddess stands on a wheel behind which is a rudder, and she holds a cubit-rule and bridle. The Roman-looking Nemesis on the right wears a crown decorated with two stags and five "small images of Victory," to quote the English version of Cartari, *Images of the Pagan Gods*; she also holds out a vessel and carries a branch.

50.
Albrecht Dürer
Little Fortune
Engraving, c. 1496
National Gallery of Art
Rosenwald Collection (1943.3.3461)

Fortune's instability is emphasized here by the slender staff. As is frequently the case,

this Fortune is "blind," her eyes either closed or without pupils. The flower she holds is thought to be an *eryngium*, a symbol of luck in love. As in Dürer's *Nemesis*, or *Great Fortune* (to distinguish it from this one), the goddess has a substantial body, conveying her power, omnipotence, and instability.

51.
Thomas Carew
Coelum Britanicum
London, 1634
Sigs. D2v–D3r

Carew's masque calls for *Tyche*, the Greek goddess of fate; but the figure is named Fortune in the speech heading, and the stage direction describes the typical conflation of Occasion and Fortune. Fortune's speech compares the omnipotence attributed to her in antiquity with the later idea that she is powerful only on earth. She says that she is the earthly agent of *Astraea*, or Justice:

> *I hold her skales*
> *And weigh mens Fates out, who have made*
> *me blind,*
> *Because themselves want eyes to see my causes,*
> *Call me inconstant, 'cause my workes surpasse*
> *The shallow fathom of their human reason.*

52.
Heinrich Oraeus
Viridarium Hieroglyphico-morale
Frankfurt, 1619
Sig. Q2v: "Fortuna moderate utendum":
"Fortune must be used with moderation"

The conflation of Fortune with Occasion is particularly apparent in this emblem of a figure, called Fortuna in the accompanying verse, which has the bald head, forelock, and razor of Occasion but the wings and veil of Fortune. She stands on an hourglass which

53

53 (detail)

is on a globe. The arrow in her hand perhaps indicates her ability to do harm, but it may also allude to Cupid, another figure who attacks at random. The verse reads,

Behold, the likeness of Fortune who wanders
  about on a rolling ball.
And easily turns and runs.
Thus, the glory and honors of the world fade;
And Humility wins the prize of heaven's heights.

53.
Niccolò Perotti
Cornucopiae
Basel, 1532
Title page

Hans Holbein engraved this "Table of Cebes," illustrating the choices humans must make between goods and the Good. In the lower right corner is a winged "Fortuna" standing on her unstable sphere. She holds a bridle, here symbolizing bad fortune, as the huddled figures below it suggest, and a covered goblet, symbolizing the good fortune of those beneath it. Since both of these accoutrements traditionally belong to Nemesis, their presence here may suggest that those who follow the path of Fortune rather than Virtue will be punished or rewarded without regard to merit.[13]

54

55

57

58

Printers' devices

The following printers' devices, found on the title pages or the final leaves of the books they are from, all belonged to continental printers. The Fortune-Occasion conflation is particularly apparent in some of these images, which were probably chosen because they would be both attractive and easily recognized. Whether the printers also saw these emblems as good luck talismans for their books is impossible to say.

54.
Printer's device of Nicolò Moretti
In, Giulio Cesare Capaccio
Il secretario
Venice, 1599
Title page: "Non Bis": "Not twice"

In this detailed image, Fortune is on the sea and holds a sail, suggesting that she is the mast and is needed to catch the wind. God's ultimate control is present, however, in the hand from the clouds on the left.

55.
Printer's device of Andreas Cratander
In, Orpheus
Argonautica
Basel, 1523
Sig. 04v

Engraved by Hans Holbein, Cratander's device represents Fortune on a sphere and wearing a veil, but she has the razor, winged feet, bald head, and forelock of Occasion.

56.
Printer's device of Giacomo Ruffinelli
In, Ascanio de' Mori
Givoco Piacevole
Mantua, 1580
Title page

Fortune is again represented on the sea, with a forelock and flowing hair, holding a billowing veil like a sail and riding through the water with one foot on a dolphin, one on a sphere.

57.
Printer's device of Comino Ventura
In, Vitale Zuccolo
Discorsi del molto
Bergamo, 1588
Title page

A rather masculine Fortune is shown on the sea, with blowing hair, billowing veil or sail, and riding on a dolphin. The sun rising on the left furthers the sense of the motto on the frame: "Bona Fortunæ": "The goods of Fortune."

58.
Printer's device of Joannes Bellerus
In, Giovanni Michele Bruto
De rebus a Carolo V Caesare
Antwerp, 1555
Sig. F8r:"Ferient Ruinae Si Fractus Illabatur Orbis Impauidum": "Were the vault of heaven to break and fall upon him, its ruins would smite him undismayed"[14]

This elaborate device shows a ship sinking in a storm while a man in the sea reaches out to Fortune, who is on dry land.

59.
Printer's device of Pietro de Franceschi
In, Orazio Toscanella
Discorsi cinque
Venice, 1575
Title page
See Astington, fig. 5

Naked Fortune holding the sail acts as the mast of a boat labeled "Regina Virtus." Virtue, crowned and holding her sceptre, is at the tiller, illustrating how Fortune and Virtue should work together.

IV.

The Height of Fortune

"A thousand moral paintings can I show
That shall demonstrate these quick blows of Fortune's
More pregnantly than words."

(William Shakespeare, *Timon of Athens*, 1.1)

In his *Dictionarie of the French and English Tongves* (1611), Randall Cotgrave gives a definition for *fortune* that is broader than the modern one: "hap, chaunce, luck, lot, hazard, aduenture; also destinie, fatall necessitie." This range from chance to inevitability left a lot of room for interpretation in terms of both human choices and artistic representation. Perhaps as a consequence, by the mid to late sixteenth century, at the height of the Renaissance in England and northern Europe, Fortune had become more an emblematic encapsulation of certain accepted ideas than a goddess with an influence on the world. The unpredictability of events had come to be seen as an inescapable fact of life. At the same time, a period of economic growth, fed partly by the exploration and exploitation of new territories in the Americas and the Far East, had fostered the optimistic belief that bad fortune could be prevented and good fortune created. Not surprisingly, when Fortune was no longer perceived as a constant and uncontrollable threat to human happiness, representations of her in both the verbal and visual arts became clichéd, repetitive, and conventional. Rather than provoking anxiety or exploring implications, they increasingly played with the idea of Fortune, or used it in a specific context, satisfying expectations, rather than challenging them.

60.
William Shakespeare
The tragicall historie of Hamlet, Prince of Denmarke
London, 1604
Sig. F1v

In the second quarto of the play, Hamlet greets Rosencrantz and Guildenstern, and they draw on the image of Fortune as a strumpet for some bawdy wordplay. The error, "Fortunes lap," is corrected to "Fortunes cap" in the 1623 First Folio.

61.
William Shakespeare
The cronicle history of Henry the fift
London, 1600
Sigs. C4v–D1r

In this exchange between Pistol and the Welsh Fluellen, every cliché about Fortune is introduced in an amusing parody of many similar serious descriptions.

62.
George Wither
A collection of emblemes ancient and modern
London, 1635
Book 3, no. XL: "Fortuna ut Luna": "Fortune is like the moon"
See Young, fig. 1

The emblems in this book are engravings by Crispijn van de Passe drawn from an earlier collection. Wither's practice, evident here with Fortune, is to give a full and satisfying summary of conventions already long associated with the figure, and to provide an explicit moral reading that emphasizes Puritan values. The linking of Fortune with the moon goes back to classical times: Fortune is like the moon in being always and quickly moving; she is the goddess who reigns in the sublunar realm, the world of change.

Opposite: From Juan de Solórzano Pereira *Emblemata regio politica*, Madrid, 1653 (cat. 78).

tifull lacke of wit, together with most weake hams, all which sir
though I most powerfully and potentlie belieue, yet I hold it not
honesty to haue it thus set downe, for your selfe sir shall growe old
as I am : if like a Crab you could goe backward.

Pol. Though this be madnesse, yet there is method in't, will you
walke out of the ayre my Lord?

Ham. Into my graue.

Pol. Indeede that's out of the ayre; how pregnant sometimes
his replies are, a happines that often madnesse hits on, which reason
and sanctity could not so prosperously be deliuered of. I will leaue
him and my daughter. My Lord, I will take my leaue of you.

Ham. You cannot take from mee any thing that I will not more
willingly part withall : except my life, except my life, except my
life. *Enter Guyldersterne, and Rosencraus.*

Pol. Fare you well my Lord.

Ham. These tedious old fooles!

Pol. You goe to seeke the Lord *Hamlet*, there he is.

Ros. God saue you sir.

Guyl. My honor'd Lord.

Ros. My most deere Lord.

Ham. My extent good friends, how doost thou *Guyldersterne*?
A *Rosencraus*, good lads how doe you both?

Ros. As the indifferent children of the earth.

Guyl. Happy, in that we are not euer happy on Fortunes lap,
We are not the very button.

Ham. Nor the soles of her shooe.

Ros. Neither my Lord.

Ham. Then you liue about her wast, or in the middle of her fa-
Guyl. Faith her priuates we. (uors.

Ham. In the secret parts of Fortune, oh most true, she is a strumpet,
What newes?

Ros. None my Lord, but the worlds growne honest.

Ham. Then is Doomes day neere, but your newes is not true;
But in the beaten way of friendship, what make you at *Elsonoure*?

Ros. To visit you my Lord, no other occasion.

Ham. Begger that I am, I am euer poore in thankes, but I thanke
you, and sure deare friends, my thankes are too deare a halfpeny;
were you not sent for? is it your owne inclining? is it a free visitati-
on? come, come, deale iustly with me, come, come, nay speake.

Guy. What should we say my Lord?

There, I do not know how you call him, but by Iesus I think
He is as valient a man as *Marke Anthonie*, he doth maintain
the bridge most gallantly : yet he is a man of no reckoning:
But I did see him do gallant seruice.

Gouer. How do you call him?

Flew. His name is ancient *Pistoll*.

Gouer. I know him not.

Enter Ancient Pistoll.

Flew. Do you not know him, here comes the man.

Pist. Captaine, I thee beseech to do me fauour,
The Duke of *Exeter* doth loue thee well.

Flew. I, and I praise God I haue merrited some loue at
(his hands.

Pist. *Bardolfe* a souldier, one of buxsome valour,
Hath by furious fate
And giddy Fortunes fickle wheele,
That Godes blinde that stands vpon the rowling restlesse
(stone.

Flew. By your patience ancient *Pistoll*,
Fortune, looke you is painted,
Plind with a musler before her eyes,
To signifie to you, that Fortune is plind :
And she is moreouer painted with a wheele,
Which is the morall that Fortune is turning,
And inconstant, and variation, and mutabilities :
And her fate is fixed at a sphericall stone
Which roules, and roules, and roules :
Surely the Poet is make an excellēt descriptiō of Fortune,
Fortune looke you is and excellent morall.

Pist. Fortune is *Bardolfes* foe, and frownes on him,
For he hath stolne a packs, and hanged must he be:
A damned death, let gallowes gape for dogs,
Let man go free, and let not death his windpipe stop.

But

63.

John Dee

General and rare memorials pertayning to
the perfect arte of nauigation

London, 1577

Frontispiece

On the ship *Europa* are Queen Elizabeth I
and three men. Elizabeth holds the rudder,
and beside the ship rides Europa on a bull.
The land is defended by ships and armed
men; in the center on a fortress stands
Occasion or Fortune. She has a forelock to
be seized and holds out a wreath in one
hand as she beckons with the other to those
who would succeed. St. Michael descends
from sun, moon, and stars. The Greek
around the frame describes the picture as
a "British Hieroglyphick." The main point is
that Britain is to seize the occasion to grow
strong at sea and further her imperial ambi-
tions; "Res-publica Britannica" is the kneeling
figure praying to rule the waves.[15]

64.

Stephen Harrison

The arches of triumph

London, 1604

No. 5: "*Hortus Euporiae*" (The Garden of
Plenty) in Cheapside

See Kiefer, fig. 2

William Kip's engraving illustrates one of
seven arches built in 1604 for the London
pageants celebrating King James I's triumphal
entry into the City as the new monarch.
Stephen Harrison designed the arches,
and Thomas Dekker wrote the pageants
performed at them. Atop the highest dome
is Fortune; in the space below are Peace
(with caduceus) and Plenty (with cornucopia). Clearly, the dominant idea here is
Fortune's benevolence.

63

65

Of loue, fortune and the louers minde. 99.

Loue, fortune, and my mynde, which do remēber
Eke that is now, and that once hath bene,
Torment my hart so sore that very often
I hate and enuy them beyond all measure,
Loue fleeth my hart while fortune is depriuer
Of al my comfort, the foolish minde than
Burneth and plaineth, as one that very seldome
Liueth in rest, So still in displeasure
My pleasant dayes they flete and passe.
And dayly doth mine yll change to the worse,
While more then halfe is runne now of my course,
Alas not of stele, but of brittle glasse,
I see that from myhand falleth my trust,
And all my thoughts ar dashed into dust.

67

68

65.
Stephen Harrison
The arches of triumph
London, 1604
No. 6: *"Cosmos Neos"* (The New World) in Fleet Street

On this arch Fortune is in the middle, standing on the sphere.

66.
Thomas Dekker
The magnificent entertainment
London, 1604
Sigs. H3v–H4r

Dekker explicates the meaning of the New World arch. Fortune is placed relative to other goddesses; at the top is *Astraea*, or Justice: *Directly under her, in a Cant by herselfe, was Arate (vertue) inthronde, her garments white, her head crowned, and vnder her Fortuna: her foote treading on the Globe, that moude beneath her: Intimating, that his Majesties fortune, was aboue the world, but his vertues aboue his fortune.*

67.
Sir Thomas Wyatt
"Of Loue, Fortune, and the louers mind"
In, *Songes and sonets* [*Tottel's Miscellany*]
London, 1574
Sig. E4r

In Wyatt's sonnet the lover laments his downfall and suffering caused by the combined forces of Love, Fortune, and his mind. The poem dwells on the contrast between his happy past and sad present, ending with an image of falling and death.

68.
Otto van Veen
Amorum emblemata
Antwerp, 1608
Sig. V3r: "Et Cum Fortuna Statque Caditque Fides": "Who stands by Fortune lets faith fall"

A blindfolded Fortune with her billowing sail and rudder, one foot on a sphere, one on land, puts a blindfold on Cupid, who stands on the sphere. The English version of the verse is titled "Blynd fortune blyndeth love":

Sometyme blynd fortune can make love bee
  also blynd,
And with her on her globe to turne & wheel
  about,
When cold prevailes to put light loves faint
  fervor out,
But fervent loyall love may no such fortune
  fynde.

EMBLEMATA. 15

Nihil ignavis votis.

EMBLEMA V.

Rebus in humanis noſtrum ſolamen opemque
Nil juvat ignavâ ſollicitare prece;
Audentes Fortuna juvo: conamina veſtra
Iungite, & hoc noſtrum præſto erit auxilium.

COMMENTARIVS.

PRoverbio celebratum eſt apud Lacedæmonios; Admotâ
manu Fortunam eſſe invocandam : Quo ſignificabant ſic
eſſe invocandos Deos ut ſimul & manum apponamus, &
noſtram addamus operam, alioqui fruſtrà invocari. Non
enim votis neque ſupplicationibus muliebribus auxilia Deo- Salluſt.
rum parantur, ſed vigilando, agendo, bene conſulendo omnia
proſ-

69

69.
Florent Schoonhoven
Emblemata
Gouda, 1618
No. 5: "Nihil ignavis votis": "Nothing
happens through useless prayers"

Fortune is pictured with forelock and billowing veil, one foot on a sphere, the other
on a wheel, all emphasizing the instability
which the men pleading for her attention
seem to ignore but of which the stormy sea
and sinking ship in the background are
reminders. The verse below can be translated,

In human affairs it is to no avail to entreat
our consolation and help with useless prayer;
I, Fortune, help those who have shown daring:
Join your attempts, and our help will be
at hand.

70.
Richard Brathwait
Times curtaine drawne
London, 1621
Sigs. N2v–N3r

In this collection of his early work, the
author satirizes contemporary social foibles
and frailties. *Panedone: or Health from
Helicon* contains "Upon Fortune," the first
half of which deals dismissively with the
goddess and her powers:

Fortune, who calls thee *blinde is not to blame,*
For so much is imported by thy name;
Worth thou respects not: he that doth inherit
Thy blind estate is one of least demerit;
Who knows not worth, but's wont to derogate
From style of Man, to better his estate.
Fondling that fawnes on greatnesse, I detest

THE ARGVMENT.

T *he ficknesse hot, a master quit, for feare,*
H *is house in towne : and left one servant there.*
E *ase him corrupted, and gave meanes to know*
A *cheater, and his punque ; who, now brought low,*
L *eaving their narrow practise, were become*
C *os'ners at large : and, onely wanting some*
H *ouse to set vp, with him they here contract,*
E *ach for a share, and all begin to act.*
M *uch company they draw, and much abuse,*
I *n casting figures, telling fortunes, newes,*
S *elling of flyes, flat bawdry, with the stone:*
T *ill it, and they, and all in fume are gone.*

PROLOGVE.

ORTVNE, that favours fooles, these two
short houres
We wish away; both for your sakes, and
ours,
Iudging Spectators : and desire in place,
To th'Author iustice, to our selues but
grace.
Our *Scene* is *London,* 'cause we would make
knowne,
No countries mirth is better then our
owne.
No clime breeds better matter, for your whore,
Bawd, squire, impostor, many persons more,

Ee 3   Whose

71

---

140   EMBLEMES NOVVEAUX.

Du calomniateur grande est la tromperie.

QUiconque va cercher son heur sur l'escrevice,
    Merveille ce sera s'il y parvient jamais :
    Il en prend tout ainsi à qui croid au mauvais,
Ou qui attend de lui quelque loyal service.

Declara-

72

To be by thee or thy vaine fauours blest;
For if I should, who liue in Wisedomes Schoole,
Would gather hence I were some brain-sicke
    foole
That had no meanes (for so they would
    report me)
But iust as purblinde Fortune did support me.

71.
Ben Jonson
The Workes
London, 1616
Sig. 2E3r

The prologue of Jonson's play *The Alchemist* begins by wishing away "Fortune, that favours fools." The printer, William Stansby, conveniently owned an initial incorporating the conventional Fortune, naked, holding a sail, and standing on a sphere.

72.
Andreas Friedrich
Emblemes Nouueaux…mis en
lumiere par Jacques de Zettre
Frankfurt, 1617
Page 140: "Du calomniateur grande est la tromperie": "Great is the deception of the slanderer"

The common image of Fortune as the mast of a ship is used by the artist of this bizarre emblem, in which the goddess rides on a

crab steered by a devil-like figure. The verse can be translated,

Whoever seeks his fortune on a crayfish,
It will be a wonder if he ever finds it:
He responds as he who believes in the evil one
Or who expects from him some loyal assistance.

73.
Allegory of Fortune
Engraving, Italian, sixteenth century
National Gallery of Art
Andrew W. Mellon Fund (1977.80.1)

Here Fortune has her familiar wings and globe, and she holds a small child, a personification of Love. The inscription reads: "I am good fortune, I have love with me. If you know me, I will make you a Gentleman." The horse, usually a symbol of the passions, is not a threat for the moment; but there are suggestions, in the horse's stance and the crumbling wall, of the impermanence of all the worldly goods Fortune offers.

74.
Simone Cantarini
Fortune
Etching, c. 1635/1636
National Gallery of Art
Ailsa Mellon Bruce Fund (1971.37.40)

This is a more lighthearted depiction of the Fortune-Love association, but uncertainty and instability are still factors, implied by the forelock which Cupid grabs and the sphere upon which Fortune rests the front of one foot. The inverted pouch from which coins fall probably suggests both the brevity of what the goddess represents and her control over what she bestows.

73

75.
Johann Ladenspelder
Venus/Fortune
Engraving
National Gallery of Art
Rosenwald Collection (1950.1.87)

The complex iconography of this print
conflates Fortune and Venus, who are usually
enemies. This figure seems not to be looking
in the direction she tells Cupid to shoot his
arrow of Love. Note that one foot rests on
a small sphere, which is itself on the end of
the chariot, and the other rests on one of the
chariot's wheels, furthering the union of the
two goddesses.

76.
Fortuna
Statuette, bronze
National Gallery of Art
Samuel H. Kress Collection (1957.14.23)

This statuette of Fortune resembles others
of *Venus Marina* (although the shell base
here is relatively recent). The figure is naked,
with a rope extending from her left shoulder
to right thigh and held there by her right
hand. Her extended left hand has a bore-hole
which, if it were *Venus Marina*, would have
held a mirror but in this case may have held
a sail. Her hair, seemingly blown forward
by the wind, also suggests the forelock of
Occasion. The figure may possibly have
been made as the finial of an inkstand.[16]

**"Fortune, constant in nothing
but inconstancy."**
(John Lyly, *Gallathea*, 1.1)

77.
Jean Jacques Boissard
Emblematum liber
Frankfurt, 1593
No. XLVI: "Nulli Prestat Velox Fortuna
Fidem": "No man can trust swift Fortune"

The human desire for the worldly goods
Fortune offers is illustrated by the crown
and bag of gold she holds out to the three
men eagerly striding up to her. Stable for
the moment, she does not stand on the
sphere beside her feet, which are on solid
ground, or turn the wheel leaning on the
cube; but perhaps her billowing veil suggests
the wind that will soon blow good fortune
away. The castles in the detailed background
probably represent the power and other
goods the men seek, but the ships on the
water are reminders of instability. The verse
can be translated,

When fortune laughs, and, more favorable,
She comes to flatter us with offer of her gifts,
Let us stay rational and aware:
For it is then when she might be more
*   formidable.*
Yet let us not reject her pleasant favor,
When she grants it to us we must enjoy it:
One may encounter her but not hold her,
Nor prevent by advice her inevitable flight.

78.
Juan de Solórzano Pereira
Emblemata regio politica
Madrid, 1653
No. 5: "Fortuna Vitrea Est": "Fortune is
made of glass"

78

To the conventional image of unstable
Fortune holding a wheel and standing on
two spheres, with her winged feet and with
wings on her back, is added the dress made
of glass, which the motto on her scarf explicates. The verse can be translated,

Behold, look upon the spheres with which
*   Fortune turns success,*
With which she rolls the sad and the happy at
*   the same time.*
If you hold on, you should fear: she flies forth
*   on nimble wings.*
If you are wary, flee: she falls—glass—to ruin,
*   smashed,*
To what great perils is [our] Fortune of glass
*   subject.*
Alas, all too short-lived she is shattered, just
*   when she sparkles the more.*
O fortunate ones, trust not fragile glass:
Rely on your virtue; that cannot be broken.

79.
Otto van Veen
[*Emblemata Horatiana*]
Antwerp, 1612
Page 155: "Fortuna non mutat genus":
"Fortune does not change her nature"
See Young, fig. 3

The Fortune-Folly connection is pictured
here: Fortune, blindfolded, holds her rudder
and stands protectively beside an ape wearing
the robes and crown and holding the sceptre
of royalty. The background shows a Venice-
like city, suggesting that water, the ever-
changing element, poses a threat to the
buildings and land.

80.
Francis Quarles
Emblemes
London, 1635
Book 1, no. 10: "Utriusque Crepundia
Merces": "A child's toys are the prize for each"
See Young, fig. 4

The association of Fortune and Fools is
captured in the bowls metaphor of the
picture, in a biblical quotation, a Latin
epigram, an English couplet, and a poem.
Fortune holds up the prize of a fool's
cap-and-bells in the game of bowls between
Cupid and Mammon, representatives of the
love of earthly goods. The scorekeeper is
a satyr, half human, half animal. Part of the
verse reads:

Come, Reader, come; Ile light thine eye the way
To view the Prize, the while the Gamesters play;
Close by the Jack, behold Gill Fortune stands
To wave the game; See, in her partiall hands
The glorious Garland's held in open show,
To cheare the Ladds, and crowne the
    Conq'rers brow;

The world's the Jack; the Gamesters that
    contend,
Are Cupid, Mammon: That juditious Friend,
That gives the ground, is Satan; and the Boules
Are sinfull Thoughts: The Prize, a Crowne for
    Fooles.

81.
Style of Niccolò Fiorentino
Fortune with sail, on a dolphin;
Alessandro di Gino Vecchietti on obverse
Medal, bronze
National Gallery of Art
Samuel H. Kress Collection (1957.14.884.b)
"Arideat Vsque": "Let him mock forever"

Fortune with a sail rides on a dolphin over
the waves; in the water is a radiant reflection
of the sun. This is the only recorded specimen
of this medal.

82.
Giulio Cesare Capaccio
Delle imprese trattato
Naples, 1592
Book 3, page 19: "Amico dell' una, & dell'
altra Fortuna": "Friend of the one, & the
other's Fate"

This unusual emblem shows Good Fortune
on the left, with billowing sail and raised
forelock, and Bad Fortune on the right, with
torn sail and forelock falling. The ship sailing
on the sea and the rising sun in the background on the "good" side, are matched by
the sinking ship and, presumably, dark night
over a city on the other.

81

83.
Fortunes tennis-ball
London, 1640
Frontispiece

In a variation on the theme of what happens
to Fortune's victims, the crude woodcut
shows a "Tree of Fortune" with the nude
goddess at the top and men falling off
below. The text of the pamphlet is headed
"Pride will have a fall." A verse on the next
page explicates the image:

See for the Fronticepiece here a Cedar tree,
Whereon sits Fortune in her Majestie.
Those that presume t' aspire unto its top,
She slilie gives the highest branch a lop,
And topsie turvie they come tumbling down,
As dazled with the brightnesse of her crown.
You that look on the root, pray look no higher
Then its true Motto, Cease too high t' aspire.

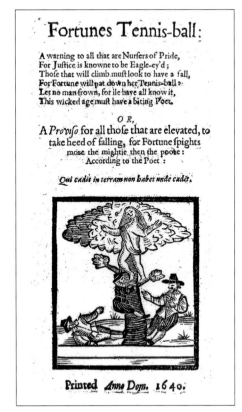

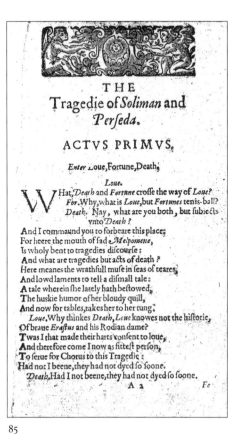

82

83

85

The appearances of Fortune as a character in Elizabethan and Jacobean plays are described in the accompanying essay by Frederick Kiefer.

84.
Thomas Dekker
The pleasant comedie of Old Fortunatus
London, 1600
Sigs. A3v–A4r
See Kiefer, fig. 3

Fortune makes a grand emblematic entrance in this play, after which there is a song about her fickleness.

85.
[Thomas Kyd]
The tragedie of Solimon and Perseda Wherein is laide open, Loues constancie, Fortunes inconstancie, and Deaths triumphs
London, 1599
Sig. A2r

This play begins with a debate among Love, Fortune, and Death, who battle for control until the end when, of course, Death wins.

86.
R. A.
The valiant Welshman
Ascribed to Robert Armin
London, 1615
Sigs. A3v–A4r

Fortune begins this play by descending from above, giving a visual dimension to the idea that she is a goddess. Similarly, having her speak the Prologue suggests that she will be in charge of the action. Her analogy between the stage and life is given in terms of Tragedy and Comedy, or bad and good Fortune.

Fortune in Shakespeare's *King Lear*

Alan R. Young, *Acadia University*

Allusions to Fortune and to Fortune's wheel are abundant in Shakespeare. They derive, as has been well documented, from a complex classical and medieval heritage, and their appearance in Shakespeare's plays often seems like the expression of a commonplace that in at least one instance (*Henry V*, 3.6.25–38) even has the semblance of laughable cliché.[1] The iconography of Fortune has also been well demonstrated by art and literary historians, so that Shakespeare scholars are generally familiar with pictures of Fortune and Fortune's wheel and the manner in which these images complement and help elucidate Shakespeare's textual allusions. Familiar too are the related and interconnected iconographic features of Occasio, Ixion's wheel, and the Circle of Life. My purpose here is not primarily to comment further upon Shakespeare's iconographic and literary heritage regarding the allusions to Fortune in *King Lear*. Rather, my aim is to offer some views about how Shakespeare employs allusions to Fortune in this play to form part of a rich visual and textual complex having to do with certain key questions that permeate the play. Of prime importance to my argument is the manner in which a steady pattern of allusions to Fortune that show instability, unpredictability, deceptiveness, and destructive potential

serves to undermine and destabilize assumptions about the natural order and the beneficence of divine power.

The key questions I have just referred to are familiar to students of the play for they are the focus for much critical discussion of *King Lear*:

1. What is the nature of Nature? and is there a relationship between cause and effect? Does so-called unnatural behavior in humans have sequent negative effect? Is there order within Nature, however imperfect?

2. What is the nature of God (or the gods)? Is divine providence beneficent, malicious, uncaring, just? And, in connection with this last, why is the suffering of some characters more than they can possibly have deserved?

3. Is the play broadly affirmative in its answers to the above two matters? Or is it pessimistic, a dramatization of nihilism? Or is it open-ended, ambiguous, unresolved? Also familiar to students of the play is the way in which the principal characters appear to divide with regard to their responses to the questions just referred to. There are the traditionalists, espousing feudal values (Lear, Gloucester, Cordelia, Kent, Albany, Edgar, the Fool) who appear to believe in a providential order of Nature and of the divine that from the human standpoint involves a mosaic of interrelated and reciprocal

obligations. That such a thing as divine justice exists is a paramount belief among these characters, regardless of how humans may fail in their attempts to be arbiters of justice. By contrast, Edmund represents a stunning and radical disbelief (for some recent critics he represents the "emerging bourgeois forces" of the early seventeenth century). Edmund sees the traditional concepts of Nature and providence, including his father's concerns about recent astrological portents, as mere superstitious apologies for human weaknesses:

This is the excellent foppery of the world, that when we are sick in fortune—often the surfeits of our own behavior—we make guilty of our disasters the sun, the moon, and stars, as if we were villains on necessity, fools by heavenly compulsion, knaves, thieves, and treachers by spherical predominance; drunkards, liars, and adulterers by an enforc'd obedience of planetary influence; and all that we are evil in, by a divine thrusting on. (1.2.117–26)

Opposite: Detail from George Wither,
A collection of emblemes, London, 1635 (cat. 62).

In Edmund's view, humans are governed by their own wills alone:

An admirable evasion of whoremaster man, to lay his goatish disposition on the charge of a star! My father compounded with my mother under the Dragon's tail, and my nativity was under Ursa Major, so that it follows, I am rough and lecherous. [Fut,] I should have been that I am, had the maidenl'est star in the firmament twinkled on my bastardizing.

(1.2.126–33).

Any perceived obligations and restraints derive from convention merely; they are not part of the "natural" state of humankind. Less articulate, perhaps, is the pragmatism of Goneril and Regan who reject traditional bonds in part out of self-preservation ("We must do something, and i' th' heat" 1.1.308) and in part out of ambition.

Interpretations of the play, and in particular answers to the three groups of questions outlined above, have in the past, like the two main groups of characters, also tended to give the appearance of being split into two main camps, one camp suggesting that the play offers some form of positive, redemptive, even Christian viewpoint, the other arguing that the play is pessimistic, even nihilistic. At their most extreme, the opposed views, according to G. R. Hibbard, are represented by "two extremes of sentimental wishful thinking and reductive nihilistic rant." As Richard Levin has recently argued, the broad critical debate between these two camps, whatever the differences between them, for long operated, in spite of all differences, within "a general agreement on the basic moral values of the play," but Marxist, cultural materialist, feminist, and new historicist critics have contributed to the undermining of such previous consensus. Also to be taken into account regarding the

wide range of critical discourse that now surrounds the play (and let us not forget the growing acceptance that there are two *King Lears*)[2] is the view outlined by David L. Kranz that the play is *intentionally* "ambiguous and unresolved, however dark in action or light in suggestion."[3]

Given the broad interpretive possibilities that the play currently offers, my purpose here is to ask where Fortune fits within all this. I believe the question is worth asking for two main reasons. First, Fortune and the various related tropes (Occasio, Ixion's Wheel, the Circle of Life) mentioned above are part of the nexus of allusions in *King Lear* to divine or supernatural power and the relationship of that power to the human condition. Secondly, the sheer frequency of these allusions in the play gives them telling weight.

Allusions to the divine or supernatural come primarily from Lear himself, with other key statements from Kent, Edgar, Gloucester, Cordelia, and Albany. All, in keeping with the view of the traditionalists in the play, assume the existence of the divine; what is in question is the exact nature of divine power and its relationship to humankind. Lear's oaths ("Now, by Apollo" 1.1.159) and the great curses he makes ("Hear, Nature, hear, dear goddess, hear!" 1.4.275; "All the stor'd vengeances of heaven fall / On her ingrateful top!" 2.4.162–63) show his belief in the gods and demonstrate his belief that the gods play a role in human affairs. Lear believes in the efficacy of cursing, itself a manifestation of his belief in divine justice. As the play unfolds, Lear's certainty erodes, and a note of the conditional and the interrogatory creeps into his discourse ("O heavens! / If you do love old men, if your sweet sway / allow obedience" 2.4.189–91; "Is there any cause in nature / that can make

these hard hearts" 3.6.77–78). Where Lear calls upon the gods to "Strike flat the thick rotundity o'th' world" (3.2.7) and to "Find out their enemies now" (3.2.51), Kent is notable for his belief in the beneficent nature of the divine: "The gods to their dear shelter take thee, maid" (1.1.82); "Thou out of heaven's benediction com'st / To the warm sun" (2.2.161–62). His faith remains unshakable: "It is the stars, / The stars above us, govern our conditions" (4.3.32–33). Albany, too, expresses belief in the potential of the divine to protect threatened innocence and virtue ("The gods defend her" 5.3.257). Earlier, upon hearing of the death of Cornwall, he makes clear his belief in divine justice and the "justicers" above "that these our nether crimes / So speedily can venge" (4.2.79–80). Edgar, towards the end of the drama, and (for many interpreters) in a moment of supreme dramatic irony, also maintains that "The gods are just" (5.3.171). Gloucester, on the other hand, the chief spokesperson at the opening of the play for belief in an astrological system and "sequent effects," ideas so despised by Edmund, is later reduced through his suffering to seeing divine power as non-beneficent, even malignant: "As flies to wanton boys are we to th'gods" (4.1.36), but, after reaching a state of despair and being "miraculously" preserved from his attempted suicide, he returns (another huge dramatic irony?) to placing his trust in the hands of the gods: "O you mighty gods! / This world I do renounce, and in your sights / Shake patiently my great affliction off" (4.6.34–36). For her part, Cordelia offers a model of piety, of belief in divine order and in the great bond underlying all of creation, and belief in the relationship between the human and the divine. To her the gods are "kind" (4.7.13).

The assumptions and faith represented by

many of the above statements are, as I have noted, undermined not only by the intrusion of the conditional, interrogatory, and despair-laden statements of Lear and Gloucester, but by the great attack upon traditional beliefs launched by Edmund in Act 1, scene 2, an attack reinforced by his own behavior and by the statements and subsequent behavior of Goneril and Regan. Just as striking is Shakespeare's reworking of his source material to create a disturbing ending during which Cordelia's forces lose the battle rather than win it,[4] King Lear is not restored to the throne but instead must confront the apparently undeserved and unjust death of Cordelia and perhaps return to madness, and Albany suggests, in spite of all that has happened, that the rule of the kingdom should be divided (5.3.320–21). It is little wonder that as far back as Samuel Johnson, many critics have found the play disturbing and, in religious terms, lacking in reassurance concerning the nature of the divine and in particular of divine justice. The heroic efforts of Romantic and Post-romantic critics to see the play as some form of redemptive paradigm have now been severely undermined by more recent critical writings so that ambiguity, instability, and uncertainty seem central to the experience of the play. What I would like to argue here is that by including allusions to Fortune in his play, Shakespeare has further added to this effect.

In King Lear there are twenty-five uses of the word "fortune" or derivatives of it, a figure similar to several other plays.[5] What matters most to my argument here are the three (or possibly four) specific allusions in King Lear to Fortune's wheel, and, from among the uses of the word "fortune," the nine instances in which Fortune is personified.[6] An examination focusing primarily upon these allusions to Fortune's wheel and

to personified Fortune reveals, I would argue, that their inclusion in King Lear undermines and destabilizes any assumptions about divine order and justice held by Shakespeare's characters and/or his audience. Glancing briefly at the history of the concept of Fortune indicates why this might be so. One might begin with Pliny, who, though not a Christian, had in the first century disparaged the cult of Fortune that he perceived around him because the attribution of either good or ill to Fortune led to detraction from the hegemony of God.[7] Imbued with the rationalist's mistrust of Providence, Pliny argued that belief in gods without number and in gods corresponding to human vices and virtues was the height of folly. In particular, Fortune was an invention attributable to human concerns about mortality, a goddess, he complained, who was everywhere invoked.[8] Such a view was shared by Augustine (after his conversion) and by Boethius, though his stance was more complex than Augustine's. While Christian writers and artists generally in the Middle Ages were often ambivalent or perceived Fortune as merely an agent of God's will,[9] Calvin and other Protestant reformers later strongly repudiated the concept of Fortune in favor of a God who foreknows and governs everything without the aid of intermediary forces. Dante's view of Fortune as somehow acting as a divine agent of providential will is thus rejected.[10] The appearance of chance, moreover, is mere appearance as far as the Reformers are concerned; nothing occurs without its being part of the will and design of God. None the less, the vitality of Fortune endured at the time of Shakespeare as a means, perhaps, of providing an explanation (even consolation) for mutability and apparently undeserved suffering, for a providence that, if it existed, was incomprehensible, and for a God whose justice

seemed arbitrary and blind to human needs and virtues. The concept of Fortune thus held the potential within a Christian belief system to offer a subversive threat to officially-sanctioned theological codes,[11] one noted in 1603 in the translation of Plutarch's Morals by Philemon Holland, who complained about those who "would needs take from God the dispose and government of humane affaires, holding and maintaining this point: That all things roll and run at a venture, and that there is no other cause of the good and evil accidents of this life, but either fortune or els the will of man" (p. 538).[12] My point will be, then, that in King Lear allusions to Fortune are among the chief causes of uncertainty and ambivalence and are strong enough to keep in check any clear expression of faith in a beneficent, all-knowing, and all-controlling divinity.

Fortune as a Wheel (or Fortune Turning a Wheel)

When Kent makes the first reference in King Lear to the Wheel of Fortune, he is, as many commentators have noted, at what seems to him the lowest point in his fortunes. An earl, now wearing a lowly disguise, sleeping in the open, subjected to the indignity of the stocks, and (symbolically perhaps) in a near prone position, he calls upon Fortune: "Fortune, good night; smile once more, turn thy wheel" (2.2.173). Virtuous man that he is, he counters Fortune's blows by taking refuge in hope. The wheel having turned and brought him from the heights of privilege to his new lowly state, he appears to assume that the wheel will continue to turn and, he hopes, bear him aloft once more. As often in this play, however, irony intervenes, as first Edgar enters, and in dire peril of his life symbolically strips off his clothes and all they signify and transforms himself into

a mad beggar. Then Lear appears, reduced to an entourage composed of only the Fool and a Gentleman (Folio) or Knight (Quarto). None of the three principal figures (Kent, Edgar, Lear) who appear in this scene have yet reached the lowest point.[13] Kent's hope is misplaced, and when the Fool advises him to "Let go thy hold when a great wheel runs down hill lest it break thy neck with following it; but the great one that goes upward, let him draw thee after" (2.3.71–74), that irony is underscored since Kent cannot be so sure of Fortune as to know with any certainty where he is placed upon the wheel. The personified Fortune that Kent addresses when he says "turn thy wheel" is, after all, constant, true, and trustworthy only in her inconstancy, falsity, and untrustworthiness, a blind goddess who stands upon a "rolling, restless stone," her wheel signifying fickleness, turning, inconstancy, mutability, and variation (*Henry V*, 3.6.29–36). Kent's initial hope and optimism are undercut, revealing either his naïveté or his blind faith in the face of adverse and inexplicable circumstances.

Later, Lear, symbolically dressed in new clothes,[14] is reunited with Cordelia. He is raised, as he puts it, "out o' th' grave" (4.7.44), a telling image of one who has touched the lowest depths of human experience and is now in the company of "a soul in bliss" (4.7.45). He is also addressed as "my royal lord," "your Majesty," and "your Highness" (4.7.43, 82) to signify the restoration of his regal status and to signify that he is now in his "own kingdom" (75). Lear, however, protests against the change ("You do me wrong…I am a very foolish fond old man" 44, 59). Although Cordelia appears to him as a heavenly creature, "a soul in bliss," he associates himself with hell, using a powerful wheel image:

> I am bound
> *Upon a wheel of fire, that mine own tears*
> *Do scald like molten lead.*
>
> (4.7.45–47)

An audience familiar with the King Lear story, the earlier play of *King Leir*, and/or the folklore analogues of the story, as I have argued elsewhere, would upon first viewing this scene recognize the opening notes of the familiar romance ending—Lear will be restored to his daughter and to his throne, and evil will be vanquished. Lear, however, has chosen to use a familiar visual symbol associated with the fires of hell and with the fate of the tortured Ixion.[15] His image, though understandable for one so confused and one who is suffering the pangs of guilt and humility, is inappropriate, or so one would feel if one expected Shakespeare to follow his sources and show Lear's restored fortunes, his reunion with his beloved daughter, his forthcoming victory in the battle, and his natural death of old age after resuming his kingship, a death that preceded that of Cordelia.[16] The only appropriate wheel image would be that of Fortune's Wheel, with Lear now being drawn upwards from his miserable and lowly state towards his true kingly and paternal role. The shock that Shakespeare administered to such expectations, of course, was to have Lear lose the battle, to have Cordelia die *before* her father, and to have one final allusion to clothing: "Pray you undo this button" (5.3.310; see note 14). This last reverses the symbolic sequence of Lear's undressing while in his mad state during the storm and his later being dressed in new clothes when he is reunited with Cordelia.[17] Significantly, Shakespeare has the final scene begin with Cordelia and Lear being led off to prison and Cordelia's allusion to

herself and her father being victims of "false Fortune's frown" (5.3.6). Built into what follows is a painful irony: her faith that she "could else out-frown false Fortune's frown" (i.e., withstand being cast down by Fortune if it was only she in trouble) is itself false for she is shortly to die, the most telling and deeply troubling example in *King Lear* of a seeming lack of divine justice, since she is innocent and her death undeserved.

The final wheel image to be noted here is that used by Edmund in the last scene of the play. Prone on the ground (according to stage and editorial traditions) after his defeat in single combat, he asks his adversary to reveal his identity ("But what art thou / That hast this fortune on me?" 5.3.165–66). This first reference to fortune from one who has so strenuously denied such supernatural forces may be of no significance, a mere turn of phrase, but when Edmund agrees with Edgar's contention that "The gods are just, and of our pleasant vices / Make instruments to plague us" (5.3.171–72), something unexpected is happening. This is further confirmed by Edmund's totally uncharacteristic reference to his fallen state in terms of Fortune: "The wheel is come full circle, I am here" (5.3.175).[18] The idea that Fortune's Wheel has now brought him to the lowest state is further enforced when the bodies of Goneril and Regan are brought on stage and perhaps placed beside him. But if Fortune has brought this trio so low, the expectation is that their principal victims, Lear and Cordelia, should by the same turning wheel have been raised. But not so. As Edmund is carried off ("Bear him hence awhile" 5.3.257), Lear enters with the dead Cordelia.[19] The promise of Act 4, scene 7, is totally dissipated, and Lear who earlier saw himself as the "fool of fortune" (4.6.190–91) is now described by Kent in even stronger terms: "If Fortune

brag of two she lov'd and hated, / One of them [i.e. Lear] we behold" (5.3.281–82). Lear's death, which follows shortly after, in a state of what appears to many viewers as bewilderment, shock, despair even, negates any cathartic promise implicit in the concept of divine justice. The references to Fortune as the play closes are especially appropriate because, though Fortune may raise one up or cast one down, it is a totally arbitrary process, and those cast down are not necessarily raised up; the wheel may turn (as in the case of Edgar and Edmund), but it may not (as in the case of Lear and Cordelia).

Other References to Fortune:
In the previous section on the Wheel of Fortune, several other references to Fortune in *King Lear* have been mentioned in passing. In conclusion, I would like to point out two more, each of which underscores the idea of Fortune as unreliable, unstable, deceptive, and unjust.

Fortune as a Whore
Traditionally, Fortune is female and, though often described as a goddess, is far more frequently dubbed with the stereotyped weaknesses attributed to the female: she is changeable (and consequently often associated with the moon—see fig. 1, cat. 62),[20] she is fickle in assigning favors, she is a seductive temptress (see fig. 2) who entraps her victims with her body, a conceit often emblematized by representing her as a beautiful nude, and at her worst she is no better than the harlot who offers her favors to all yet readily deceives all, a common Latin epithet for her being "meretrix".[21] Shakespeare was clearly aware of the motif of Fortune as whore.[22] At one point in *King John*, Constance addresses her son Arthur and speaks of how at his birth "Nature and Fortune join'd to make

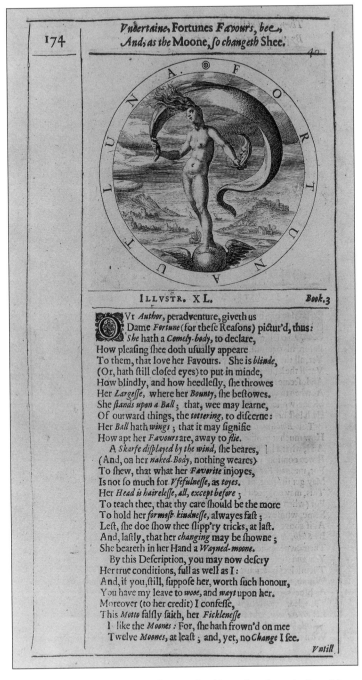

Fig. 1: From George Wither, *A collection of emblemes*, London, 1635 (cat. 62).

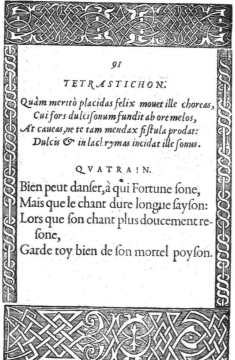

Fig. 2: From Guillaume de la Perrière, *La Morosophie*, Lyons, 1553.

thee great" (3.1.52). Now, however, matters have changed; Fortune is an adulteress and a whore:

> But Fortune, O,
> She is corrupted, chang'd, and won from thee;
> Sh'adulterates hourly with thine uncle John,
> And with her golden hand hath pluck'd on
>   France
> To tread down fair respect of sovereignty,
> And made his majesty the bawd to theirs.
> France is a bawd to Fortune and King John,
> That strumpet Fortune, that usurping John!
>   (3.1.54–61)

In *Hamlet*, the first meeting of Hamlet with Rosencrantz and Guildenstern, in parody of the bonhomie of male college students,

immediately elicits a series of bawdy allusions to Fortune's "secret parts" (2.2.235), Hamlet bringing the interchange to an end by remarking that "she is a strumpet" (2.2.236). Elsewhere in *Hamlet*, the Player in his description of the death of Priam declaims:

> Out, out, thou strumpet Fortune! All you gods,
> In general synod take away her power!
> Break all the spokes and [fellies] from her wheel,
> And bowl the round nave down the hill of heaven
> As low as to the fiends!
>   (2.2.493–97)

And in *Macbeth*, as the play opens, the Sergeant describes how in the battle Fortune initially favored Macdonwald until Macbeth killed him:

> And Fortune, on his damned [quarrel] smiling,
> Show'd like a rebel's whore. But all's too weak;
> For brave Macbeth (well he deserves that name),
> Disdaining Fortune, with his brandish'd steel....
>   (1.2.14–17)

In *King Lear*, a play in which the less positive characteristics of Fortune seem most apparent, it is hardly surprising that the same motif appears. Significantly, the motif occurs in Act 2, in the extended scene (see note 13) in which Kent sits in the stocks. The Fool sings to Lear a painfully appropriate song about the blunt realities of the economic relationship that normally binds children to parents, a relationship that Lear has now destroyed by altering the customary balance of financial power:

> Fathers that wear rags
> Do make their children blind,
> But fathers that bear bags
> Shall see their children kind.
>   (2.4.48–51)

The snatch of song then ends with the couplet

> Fortune, that arrant whore,
> Ne'er turns the key to th' poor.
>   (52–53)

To some extent, as at the beginning of the play where Cordelia mars her fortunes (1.1.95), where Burgundy's love is revealed as mere "respects of fortune" (248), and where France receives her (in the words of Goneril's pun) "At fortune's alms" (278), the ideas of fortune as material benefit and as the personified figure that has the potential to bestow benefit are conflated. In the Fool's words is the usual assumption that Fortune is a whore, and hence deceiving and untrustworthy. A new twist is given to the commonplace, however, by the Fool's reminder that whores do not open the door to those in poverty, the implication being that Lear,

who is now poor, will be denied the benefits of Fortune.[23] It is surely darkly ironic, then, that at this very moment Lear uses an image of climbing, but he talks not of the promise of the restoration of material fortune but of his inner psychological state:

O how this mother swells up towards my heart! [Hysterico] passio, *down, thou climbing sorrow, Thy element's below.*

(2.4.56–58)

The Fool as Fortune's Victim

A familiar commonplace to Shakespeare and his contemporaries was encapsulated in the proverb "Fortune favors fools" or its Latin ancestor *Fortuna favet fatuis* (see cat. 71 and figs. 3 and 4).[24] Erasmus wittily exploited the idea in his *Moriae Encomium* (1515) when Folly begins a short discussion of her relationship with Fortune by saying: "Fortune, the directrix of human affairs, favors me while she has always been very hostile to the wise, because she gives all her rewards to fools, even while they are asleep" (160). The adage is also aptly dramatized in W. Wager's *The Longer Thou Livest, the More Fool Art Thou* (c. 1559–1568), in which is presented the life story of Moros (the Fool). Fortune in this play, as a means of demonstrating her power over human affairs, deliberately bestows her gifts upon Moros, calling upon the willing collaboration of such vices as Incontinence, Wrath, Ignorance, Idleness, Impiety, and Cruelty. Ultimately, in the final part of the play, Moros is laid low by God's Judgement. Moros has been favored by Fortune, but in effect he has been misled by her and may thus be seen as her victim. This concept of the deceptive nature of Fortune's gifts that fool their recipient seems to have been in Shakespeare's mind when he has Romeo, who is newly married to Juliet but

Fig. 3: Blindfolded Fortune favoring an ape. From Otto van Veen, *Emblemata Horatiana*, Antwerp, 1612 (cat. 79).

Fig. 4: Fortune holds the prize of a fool's cap. From Francis Quarles, *Emblemes*, London, 1635 (cat. 80).

now the killer of her cousin Tybalt, recognize the full import of what has occurred. In just a few seconds all the hopes of the young lovers have been reversed. Fortune has betrayed them, or as Romeo says, "O, I am fortune's fool!" (3.1.136).[25] In *King Lear*, Lear mistakenly believes that he too has come to a terrible turning point. When in 4.6 the Gentleman enters and orders those with him to "lay hand upon" Lear (188), the intention is to lead Lear to Cordelia where he can be reunited with his daughter and cared for by her. Instead, in his madness, Lear flees, believing that he is being taken prisoner. In his horror, he says,

No rescue? What, a prisoner? I am even
The natural fool of fortune.
        (4.6.190–91)

He is suggesting that he is the born (natural) plaything (fool) of fortune. A few lines earlier he has remarked that "When we are born, we cry that we are come / To this great stage of fools" (182–83). Lear's reference to himself as "fool of fortune" inevitably then has broader implications. He speaks, as it were, for all who play parts upon "this great stage of fools," and, though he is mistaken in his reading of the facts at this point, all too soon after his reunion with Cordelia, false Fortune frowns (5.3.6), and we hear Edgar, contrary to Shakespeare's sources in the chronicles, announce defeat and the capture of father and daughter: "King Lear hath lost, he and his daughter ta'en" (5.2.6). By this stage of the play, of course, the character of the Fool has unaccountably disappeared. As far as I can discern, Shakespeare never associates the Fool with the conceit just discussed that depicts fools as victims of fortune; instead, his Fool when on stage tends to be the paradoxical representative of wisdom in a world dominated by those who lack it.

154

EMBLEMATA
XXXI. EMBLEMA.

FRANGOR PATIENTIA

XXXI. GALLICE.

Ie ne tien point cas fortuits les maux
Qu'on void souuent assaillir la personne:
Car l'affligé doit dire en tous assaux,
C'est toy, Seigneur, donc point ie ne m'estonne.
Au cœur Chrestien la foy cecy raisonne
Que Dieu fait tout par sa grand' prouidence.
L'exemple auons en Iob, saincte personne,
Tresbeau miroir de vraye patience.

XXXI. LA.

Fig. 5: From Georgette de Montenay, *Liure d'armoiries en signe*, Frankfurt, 1619 (cat. 15).

Conclusion

In the events that follow the reunion of Lear and Cordelia in 4.7, Shakespeare, playing free with his sources, engineers a bleak and destructive course of events during which the forces of evil self-destruct but during which we witness the torture of a father whose daughter, an innocent and virtuous woman, has been murdered before his eyes.[26] When seen in conjunction with earlier events, during which scarcely anyone has escaped the vicious reversals of fortune, we detect a deliberate pattern in which Fortune, so frequently referred to in the play, and aptly so on account of her unstable, unpredictable, deceptive, and potentially destructive powers, appears to have a central role, eclipsing that of any other supposed deity, within what certain critics have referred to as the upside-down world of the play.[27] The collective role of the many allusions to Fortune is to undermine and destabilize the assumptions of many of the principal characters (and, no doubt, disturb those of many auditors, both in Shakespeare's day and since) concerning natural order and the supposed beneficence of the divine power(s) that govern that order.

Notes

1. All quotations from Shakespeare are from *The Riverside Shakespeare*, 2nd edition, ed. G. Blakemore Evans (Boston: Houghton Mifflin, 1997). Quotations from Ben Jonson are from *Ben Jonson,* edited by C. H. Herford and Percy Simpson, 11 vols. (Oxford: Clarendon Press, 1925–1952). Quotations from W. Wager's *The Longer Thou Livest the More Fool thou Art* are from the edition by R. Mark Benbow (Lincoln: University of Nebraska Press, 1967). Quotations from John Webster are from *The Complete Works of John Webster*, edited by F. L. Lucas (London: Chatto & Windus, 1966).

2. It is now generally accepted that the 1608 Quarto and 1623 Folio texts of *King Lear* are to be treated as versions of perhaps equal authority, each with its own literary integrity, and each consequently worthy of separate publication, as was done in the *Oxford Shakespeare*.

3. See, G. R. Hibbard, "*King Lear*: A Retrospect, 1939–79," *Shakespeare Survey* 33 (1980), 3; Richard Levin, "*King Lear* Defamiliarized" in *Lear from Study to Stage: Essays in Criticism*, edited by James Ogden and Arthur H. Scouten (Madison, Teaneck: Fairleigh Dickinson University Press, 1997), 148; Paul Delaney, "*King Lear* and the Decline of Feudalism," *PMLA* 92 (1977), 439; and David L. Kranz, "'Is This the Promis'd End?' Teaching the Play's Conclusion" in *Approaches to Teaching Shakespeare's 'King Lear,'* edited by Robert H. Ray (New York: MLA, 1986), 136.

4. Alan R. Young, "The Written and Oral Sources of *King Lear* and the Problem of Justice in the Play." *Studies in English Literature* 15 (1975), 317.

5. There are, for example, 25 in *The Merchant of Venice*; 25 in *As You Like It*; 21 in 3 *Henry VI*; 29 in *Timon of Athens*; and 21 in *Othello.* The notable exception is *Antony and Cleopatra* which has 44. These figures are based on Marvin Spevack, *The Harvard Concordance to Shakespeare* (Cambridge, Mass.: Harvard University Press, 1973).

6. Two of these last are perhaps debatable as instances of personification. See, Edmund's "Briefness and fortune work" (2.1.18) and Edgar's "A most poor man, made tame to fortune's blows" (4.6.221).

7. For a history of attitudes to Fortune prior to Shakespeare, see Frederick Kiefer, *Fortune and Elizabethan Tragedy* (San Marino: The Huntington Library, 1983), 1–29; and Willard Farnham, *The Medieval Heritage of Elizabethan Tragedy* (Oxford: Blackwell, 1963), 110–16.

8. Invenit tamen inter has utrasque sententias medium sibi ipsa mortalitas numen, quo minus etiam plana de deo coniectatio esset: toto quippe mundo et omnibus locis omnibusque horis omnium vocibus Fortuna sola invocatur ac nominatur,…" [Nevertheless mortality has rendered our guesses about God even more obscure by inventing for itself a deity intermediate between these two conceptions. Everywhere in the whole world at every hour by all men's voices Fortune alone is invoked and named,…]. (C. Plinius Secundus, *Natural History*, with English translation by H. Rackham, The Loeb Classical Library, Volume 1 [1938; rpt. London: Heinemann, 1967], Book II v 22).

9. For an example of the later currency of this concept, see Georgette de Montenay's emblem "Frangor patientia" in *Emblemes, ou devises chrestiennes* (Lyons, 1571). See Fig. 5, cat. no. 15 (1619 ed.).

10. Dante has Virgil explain that Fortune's power is subservient to that of God and is part of the divine plan: "Similemente a li splendor mondani / ordinò general ministra e duce" (In like manner, for worldly splendors He ordained a general minister and guide). (Dante Alighieri, *The Divine Comedy: The Inferno*, translated by Charles S. Singleton, Bollingen Series LXXX, 2 vols.[Princeton: Princeton University Press, 1970], VII, 77–78).

11. See William R. Elton, *King Lear and the Gods* (San Marino: The Huntington Library, 1966). Elton sees a relationship between the idea that "providence, if it existed, had little or no relation to the particular affairs of men" and an Epicurean revival that prevailed "among those increasingly susceptible to skepticism" (p. 9). Elton's chapter on "Renaissance Concepts of Providence" is a particularly helpful account of the complexities of Renaissance beliefs concerning these matters.

12. Philemon Holland (trans.), *The Philosophie, Commonlie Called, the Morals* (1603). For other statements of this kind, all dating from the period of *King Lear*, see Elton, 17–29.

13. I share the view now common among editors that 2.2–4 is one extended scene, with Kent remaining visible on the stage in the stocks throughout.

14. Earlier in the play Lear had attempted to tear off his clothes, garments presumably that clearly indicated his royal status (3.4.108–9). As R. A. Foakes has noted in his edition of *King Lear*, Lear's new clothes in 4.7 are often white to signify humility, but possibly in early performances he was "visibly a king again" (*King Lear*, The Arden Shakespeare [Walton-on-Thames: Nelson, 1997], 20, 351). As has often been noted, Lear's symbolic changes of clothing run parallel to those of Edgar and Kent who both appear at the end of the play restored in status and, it would appear, in appropriate dress. Allusions to clothing and clothing imagery in *King Lear* provide an important theme in the play. See Robert Bechtold Heilman, *This Great Stage: Image and Structure in 'King Lear'* (Seattle: University of Washington Press, 1963), Chapter Three.

15. O. B. Hardison, "Myth and History in *King Lear*," *Shakespeare Quarterly* 26 (1975), 229; Elton, 236–37; Soellner, "*King Lear* and the Magic of the Wheel," *Shakespeare Quarterly* 35 (1984), 282. Howard Patch (*The Goddess Fortuna in Mediaeval Literature* [Cambridge, Mass.: Harvard University Press, 1927], 167) and others have pointed out that the respective Wheels of Fortune and Ixion are often linked in literature. I find particularly suggestive, however, that in the anonymous play *Lust's Dominion* (London, 1657) Eleazor at the opening of 1.4 remarks: "I am whipt, and rackt, and torn upon the wheel / Of giddy fortune."

16. Young, 316. *The True Chronicle History of King Leir*, probably first performed in the early 1590s, contains the death of neither father nor daughter. The assumption at the end of the play is that Leir will live happily ever after following his restoration. On the dating of *King Leir* and the extent to which it may have been known to the audiences of Shakespeare's *King Lear*, see W. W. Greg, "The Date of *King Lear* and Shakespeare's Use of Earlier Version of the Play," *The Library* 20 (1940), 382–84. Elton has argued that the earlier *King Leir* is permeated with Christian emphases that Shakespeare went out of his way to avoid (63–71).

17. It is usually assumed that Lear is referring to his own clothing, thereby echoing his earlier "come, unbutton here" (3.4.108–9); however, it is conceivable that he is referring to Cordelia's clothing (Foakes, 390).

18. Edmund had early in the play rejected the idea that "when we are sick in fortune" it may be due to "necessity" and "heavenly compulsion" (1.2.119–22). Edmund of course does not in 5.3 specify that the wheel he refers to is that of Fortune. It may, as Rolf Soellner has suggested, be the Wheel of Life, an iconographic motif well-known in the Middle Ages and the Renaissance, but one that may still be associated with Fortune, as in Jean Cousin's illustration of "Ultima Fortuna" which shows Death's hand on the Wheel of Life but Fortune's hand on Death's arm. See, Soellner, 283; Samuel C. Chew, *The Pilgrimage of Life* (New Haven & London: Yale University Press, 1962), 149–53; Patch, p. 173; John Erskine Hankins, *Shakespeare's Derived Imagery* (Lawrence: University of Kansas Press, 1953), 19; and Jean Cousin, *Book of Fortune (Livre de Fortune)*, edited by Ludovic Lalanne (Paris and London: Librairie de l'art, 1883).

19. If one stage door was used for Edmund's exit and another for Lear's entrance, the transition could be virtually simultaneous, an ironic visual effect to match the oral irony of Albany's "The gods defend her!" The irony that Lear enters with Cordelia's corpse immediately following (or even at the same time as) the pious Albany's statement (5.3.257) has

been noted by several commentators. For Wyndham Lewis, it was even significant evidence of the play's nihilism (179–80). Lewis refers to "the punctual arrival of Cordelia, brought in like a Christmas present, so *Narquois* and so pat" as "the poet's mockery at the vanity of human supplications and notions of benevolent powers, of whom we are the cherished children" (*The Lion and the Fox: The Role of the Hero in the Plays of Shakespeare* [London: Grant Richards, 1927], 180). Cf. A. C. Bradley, *Shakespearean Tragedy: Lectures on Hamlet, Othello, King Lear, Macbeth*, 3rd edition, [London: Macmillan, 1992], 285; Elton, 254. See also Harold Bloom's recently-published powerful argument (*Shakespeare: The Invention of the Human* [New York: Riverhead Books, 1998], 476–515) that the play is characterized by "profound nihilism" (493).

20. George Wither in *A Collection of Emblemes* (1635) includes an emblem of Fortune (see fig. 1, cat. 62). She is depicted as nude ("*She hath a Comely-body*") to please those "that love her Favours," but she is blind and likely to play "slipp'ry tricks" upon her favorites. "… her *Ficklenesse / Is like the Moones*," and indeed she holds the moon in her left hand (174). The engraved Latin motto accompanying the picture derived from Gabriel Rollenhagen (Wither used the plates from this latter's emblem book) is "*Fortuna ut luna*" (Fortune is like the moon). In another emblem, Wither depicts a woman standing upon a winged ball to denote fickleness, but a section of his *subscriptio* carefully explains that the association of fickleness with women is the misleading result of semantic conventions. On Fortune and the moon, see Patch, 50–51; Farnham, 105–8; and Chew, 39. For another emblem depicting Fortune as a seductress, see Guillaume de la Perrière's *La Morosophie* (Lyons, 1553), No. 91 (fig. 2).

21. Chew, 39; and Patch, 12, 38, 56–57. Jonson used the motif at least twice. In *Every Man Out of His Humor*, it is "the strumpet *Fortune*" (I.iii.11) and in *Catiline*, it is "the whore FORTVNE" (5.600 [5.8.9]). Lodovico at the opening of Webster's *The White Devil* remarks that "Fortun's a right whore" (1.1.4).

22. In addition to the examples cited here are those allusions to huswife Fortune (*Henry V*, 5.1.80; *As You Like It*, 1.2.31; and *Antony and Cleopatra*, 4.14.44) that convey a similar idea.

23. It has been suggested (Soellner, 281) that Shakespeare is here alluding to Fortuna Philapolis, gatekeeper and protectress of castles and towns. The commonplace nature of the "Fortune as whore" motif, together with the dramatic context in which it here appears, makes Soellner's idea somewhat unlikely in my view.

24. Shakespeare makes use of the motif in *As You Like It* when Jaques meets Touchstone in the Forest of Arden. Touchstone, the Fool, is railing upon Lady Fortune and is reported by Jaques to have said: "Call me not fool till heaven hath sent me fortune" (2.7.19). Chew provides a number of examples of the commonplace from such authors as Brathwaite, Chapman, Dekker, John Heywood, Jonson, Nashe, and Taylor the Water-poet (62–63, 325, note 9).

25. Cf. the dramatic turning point in *Timon of Athens* when the empty dishes are uncovered before Timon's fairweather friends, whom Timon calls "fools of fortune" (3.6.96).

26. Lear's "I kill'd the slave that was a-hanging thee" (5.3.275) suggests something of the horror that has happened off stage.

27. James Black, "*King Lear*: Art Upside-Down," *Shakespeare Survey* 33 (1980), 35.

Fortune on the Renaissance Stage: An Iconographic Reconstruction

Frederick Kiefer, *University of Arizona*

An artist creating a picture of Fortune may vary the usual representation by assembling her customary attributes in a new way, by highlighting some unusual feature of her personification, or even by inventing some new iconographic symbol. A playwright creating a character named Fortune will have different priorities, for in the theater the character needs to be instantly recognizable to the playgoer. On the stage, then, a novel and intriguing iconographic presentation will likely prove a liability rather than an asset. And so, although Fortune's appearance may vary from one play to another, the visual representation of Fortune remains conservative for the most part, lest the identity of Fortune seem mysterious to the playgoer.

Elizabethan Staging

One of the first appearances of Fortune on the Elizabethan stage may seem at odds with the contention that Fortune's iconography generally remains simple and straightforward in the theater. In *Jocasta*, written by George Gascoigne and Francis Kinwelmersh and performed at Gray's Inn for the Christmas revels of 1566, Fortune is at the center of the dumb show preceding the final act. The iconographic description is richly detailed:

First the stillpipes sounded a very mournful melody, in which time came upon the stage a woman clothed in a white garment, on hir head a piller, double faced, the formost face fair & smiling, the other behinde blacke & louring, muffled with a white laune [fine cloth] about hir eyes, hir lap ful of jewelles, sitting in a charyot, hir legges naked, hir fete set upon a great round bal, & being drawen in by iiij noble personages, she led in a string on hir right hand ij kings crowned, and in hir lefte hand ij poore slaves very meanly attyred.[1]

The double face, the blindfold, the jewels, and sphere—all these are commonplaces and find innumerable counterparts in the visual arts of the sixteenth century. What makes the description unusual is the appearance of Fortune in a chariot,[2] and what makes the dumb show dramatic is the action she performs as charioteer: Fortune changes "*the kings unto the left hande & the slaves unto the right hand, taking the crownes from the kings heads she crowned therwith the ij slaves, & casting the vyle clothes of the slaves upon the kings, she despoyled the kings of their robes, and therwith apparelled the slaves.*" The moral is clear enough: Fortune functions as "*a plaine type or figure of unstable fortune*"; she elevates the dejected and casts down those whom formerly she advanced. In a play

about the dangers of ambition, the pantomimic action renders sharply pointed the playwrights' admonition.

Despite the elaborate nature of this dumb show, Gascoigne and Kinwelmersh were probably taking little risk of taxing either their audience's patience or powers of interpretation, for the young men at Gray's Inn, like those at the other Inns of Court, were educated and sophisticated. Such playgoers would almost certainly have relished a proliferation of visual symbolism of the kind we find in *Jocasta*. In fact, they may well have felt that the playwrights were paying them a compliment by dramatizing a complicated iconographic program. Dramatists appealing to a broader cross section of the populace, however, could take no such chance. Esoteric or elaborate iconography might baffle and even alienate a more unsophisticated audience.

Perhaps the earliest surviving play to adopt Fortune as a speaking character is *The Longer Thou Livest, The More Fool Thou Art*, written by William Wager and performed

---

Opposite left: Detail of a many-handed and two-faced Fortune from John Lydgate's adaptation of Boccaccio's *Falles of…princes*, London, 1554 (cat. 11).

c. 1558–1568. The didacticism of this early Elizabethan play is to be seen in a plot concerned with the achievement of salvation and in characters who bear the names of abstractions. Wager's play dramatizes the history of Moros, whose youthful folly and indifference to moral counsel lead him to perdition. This emphasis on education suggests that the *The Longer Thou Livest* was written as "a school or college play."[3] Indeed, the prologue announces this purpose: "I would wish parents and masters to do what they can / Both to teach and correct their youth with reason" (ll. 33–34).[4]

When Fortune appears onstage, she exults in her defiance of reason, virtue, and justice: "A popish fool will I place in a wiseman's seat" (l. 1065). The playwright here dramatizes a popular saying, "Fortune favors fools," a notion that finds visual expression in an emblem by Otto van Veen (cat. 79; see Young, fig. 3).[5] In fact the name of the character derives from a Latin word, *moror*, meaning *to be foolish*. By ennobling the unworthy Moros, Fortune will demonstrate her power: "He shall teach you Fortune to know / And to honor her till you die" (ll. 1068–69). What would most economically and swiftly announce Fortune's identity to the playgoer is the implement that figures most prominently in the visual arts. Fortune "was presumably always identifiable by her wheel," T. W. Craik observes.[6] The actor playing Fortune could easily have rolled a wagon wheel onto the stage: "she enters alone, and so must carry her wheel herself if she has it" (p. 63). Possibly, the actor held a small wheel in the hand, as we see in Hans Sebald Beham's print (cat. 30, fig. 1).[7] So ubiquitous is Fortune in Elizabethan culture that no other symbol would be required to make her identity plain.

Fortune also appears in *The Rare Triumphs*

Fig. 1: Hans Sebald Beham, *Fortune*, Engraving, 1541 (cat. 30). Courtesy of the National Gallery of Art.

of Love and Fortune, performed by Derby's Men in the late 1580s and published in 1589. This anonymous play is probably *A History of Love and Fortune*, acted at Windsor Castle in 1582. Much less didactic than *The Longer Thou Livest*, *The Rare Triumphs* employs the materials of romance—a story of wandering and separation and accidental meetings and magic—to dramatize a love story. Fortune assumes a considerably greater role in this play than in Wager's. In fact, much of the first act is given over to the onstage contention of Fortune and Love, each of whom determines to demonstrate hegemony over humankind. In subsequent acts both Fortune and Venus return to assess the action of the love story and to claim supremacy.

Spectacle plays a much greater role in *The Rare Triumphs* than in *The Longer Thou Livest*. In the first act, for example, Jupiter commands that Mercury summon before the gods "The ghosts of them that Love and Fortune slue" (l. 205).[8] Several dumb shows ensue, complete with instrumental music. And at the conclusion of the subsequent acts, playgoers witness the "triumph" of either Fortune or Venus. Despite this spectacle, it is difficult to determine precisely how Fortune was costumed.[9] In one petulant claim of Fortune, however, we find a clue to a likely hand prop: "ye see all earthly thinges are wearing out alwaies, / As brittle as the glasse, unconstant like the minde, / As fickle as the whirling wheele, as wavering as the winde" (ll. 166–68). Following the second act, Fortune again singles out her "rowling wheele of chaunce" (l. 558) as evidence of her sovereignty. It would, of course, have been theatrically advantageous for the character actually to roll the wheel while she spoke, for some stage business would give visual form to her self-description.

Fortune also comes to the stage as a contestant in *The Tragedy of Soliman and Perseda*, probably written by Thomas Kyd c. 1588–1592.[10] The subtitle of the printed play heralds the nature of the conflict: *Wherein is laid open Love's Constancy, Fortune's Inconstancy, and Death's Triumphs.* A much darker play than *The Rare Triumphs*, Kyd's *Soliman and Perseda* dramatizes a love story that ends tragically. Here the three personifications—Fortune, Love, and Death—initiate the action by squabbling among themselves, each claiming supremacy. Their respective powers are tested on Erastus and Perseda, the would-be lovers frustrated by the emperor Soliman.

As in earlier Elizabethan plays, it seems almost certain that a wheel identified

Fig. 2: From Stephen Harrison, *The arches of triumph*, London, 1604 (cat. 64).

Fortune to the playgoers. Fortune remarks in the opening scene, "Ile…cease to turne my wheele" (l. 34).[11] Later she again cites her implement while commenting on the adventures of Erastus and Perseda: Fortune speaks of turning her "tickle [i.e., insecure, changeable] wheele" (1.6.20). And she evokes visual depictions of men actually riding her wheel when she says of Erastus that she will "lift him up, and throw him downe againe" (2.3.17). Hans Sebald Beham's engraving of Fortune, cited above, places the miniature figure of a man on her wheel.

Fortune may have carried something else besides the wheel, for she asks, "Why, what is *Love* but *Fortunes* tenis-bal?" (1.1.2). Dame Fortune here evokes a proverbial saying,[12] one that could have been made theatrically interesting if the character actually bounced a tennis ball on the stage. Such a ball would have had the advantage of evoking a principal symbol of this figure: a sphere, or globe. In the visual arts Fortune commonly stands upon a rolling sphere, symbolic of her changeable nature. It would be awkward, however, for the actor playing Fortune to haul both wheel and sphere onto the stage, and there would certainly have been no way for the actor to perch upon a sphere without sacrificing dignity, not to mention balance. The tennis ball would recall a customary symbol without presenting the practical problems involved in bringing onstage a sphere large enough to stand upon.

Two additional comments made by Fortune in *Soliman and Perseda* hint at other aspects of her appearance. In the play's opening scene Fortune tells Love and Death, "Ile stay my flight" (1.1.34). This probably signals that Fortune wears wings, a symbol of her swiftness, her fleeting quality. From antiquity poets sometimes describe a winged Fortune, and this feature became increasingly

common in the Renaissance when Fortune was conflated with Occasion, or Opportunity. As Fortune and Occasion merged, Fortune also acquired a sail, symbolic of an individual's need to accommodate himself to changing circumstance and of his capacity to capitalize on opportunity. One of the arches in the coronation procession of King James I, entitled "The Garden of Plenty," features a statue of Fortune holding the sail (cat. 64, fig. 2).[13] In Kyd's play Fortune evokes such a sail when she claims, "I fild *Erastus* sailes with winde" (4.3.12). (Heinrich Aldegrever combines Fortune and Occasion by giving Fortune a sail but depicting on the sail itself the wheel upon which figures wearing fools' caps rise and fall.[14])

Near the turn of the century Fortune appears in two plays known to have been performed at Queen Elizabeth's court. One of these, Thomas Dekker's *The Pleasant Comedy of Old Fortunatus* (cat. 84, fig. 3), was acted by the Admiral's men in November of 1599 at the Rose theater and at Richmond Palace before Queen Elizabeth on 27 December. Published in 1600, the play dramatizes the story of Fortunatus (the fortunate one) as he seeks to profit from the possession of a magic purse and hat.

With the single exception of *Jocasta*, staged a generation earlier, Dekker's comedy gives us more information about Fortune's onstage appearance than does any of the plays we have considered, for his stage directions are more complete.[15] The play's first scene, for instance, describes Fortune's entry in considerable detail: "*Enter a* Carter, *a* Tailor, *a* Monke, *a* Shepheard *all crown'd, a* Nimph *with a globe, another with* Fortunes *wheele, then* Fortune: *After her fowre* Kings *with broken crownes and scepters, chained in silver gives and led by her*" (1.1.63.s.d.).[16] Here other characters bring onstage the symbols that

identify Fortune, and Dekker employs not only a wheel but also a sphere. This object is presumably placed on the floor of the stage, for moments after her entry, Fortune asks: "Behold you not this globe, this golden bowle, / This toy cal'd worlde at our imperiall feete?" (ll. 99–100). The "bowle" represents not only the instability of Fortune but also the extent of her dominion; she conflates her rolling ball and the terrestrial globe when she says, "This world is *Fortunes* ball wherewith she sports" (l. 101).

Having other characters bear the accoutrements onstage leaves Fortune's hands free to lead by chains the captive kings, whose miserable status manifests her power. The accompanying song underscores her might: "Since heaven and hell obey her power, / Tremble when her eyes doe lowre" (1.1.68–69). Fortune's authority is manifest too when she "*takes her chaire, the* Kings *lying at her feete, shee treading on them as shee goes up*" (1.1.63.s.d.). The chair must be some kind of throne appropriate to a figure who holds monarchs in her thrall.

Dekker's staging bears a close resemblance to a scene in Christopher Marlowe's *Tamburlaine the Great*, acted c. 1587. Marlowe's conquering hero treats his captives with a Fortune-like disdain: at one point he orders, "Bring out my footstool" (4.2.1),[17] and his men produce the captive Bajazeth, emperor of the Turks. The stage direction leaves no doubt that Tamburlaine "*gets up upon him to his chair*" (l. 29.s.d.). Is Dekker remembering Marlowe's example when in *Old Fortunatus* Fortune treads on kings? It would seem that he is; in fact, Dekker includes Bajazeth as one of the four kings who are led onstage by Fortune, and she herself mentions Tambur-laine (1.1.192). There is some indication, however, that in writing *Old Fortunatus* Dekker may have

patched together and revised two earlier plays of uncertain date.[18]

Later in *Old Fortunatus* Fortune makes another appearance, her attendants again carrying her symbols: "*Fortune [enters], one bearing her wheele, another her globe*" (1.3.0.s.d.). This time Fortune does not need to have her hands free to hold anything as she did earlier, but assigning the task of carrying her accoutrements to other figures perhaps helps to preserve Fortune's majesty. The only indication of costume is a remark Fortune makes to a son of Fortunatus: "on my wings / To *England* shalt thou ride" (4.1.220–21). As we have seen, wings were a conventional part of Fortune's iconography, and so the sight of a winged Fortune would have been familiar to playgoers.

The prop that Fortune handles in *Old Fortunatus* is a magic purse, which she gives to Fortunatus: "receive this purse: with it this vertue, / Still when thou thrusts thy hand into the same, / Thou shalt draw foorth ten pieces of bright gold" (1.1.299–301). Since Fortune is the author of prosperity and since she is often pictured holding a full purse or bag of money, the playgoers could have expected to see Fortune with such an object.[19] Fortune may also have the symbolic thread of life in her hands at one point. Shortly before the death of Fortunatus we find this stage direction: "*Enter* Fortune: *after her three* Destinies *working*" (2.2.213.s.d.).[20] She tells the despondent Fortunatus, "This inckie thread thy ugly sinnes have spun, / Blacke life, blacke death; faster, that it were don" (ll. 242–43). Fortune need not actually touch the black thread, of course; she could simply point to it.[21] But it would be theatrically appropriate if the deity who earlier handed to Fortunatus the magic purse were now to hold out to him the thread of his own misspent life.

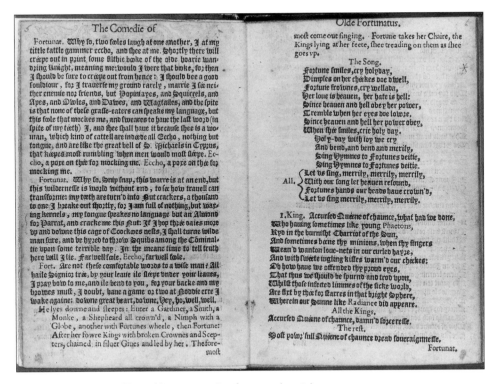

Fig. 3: From Thomas Dekker, *Old Fortunatus*, London, 1600 (cat. 84).

The version of *Old Fortunatus* that Dekker prepared for courtly performance brings Fortune back onto stage in the final scene, the playwright's purpose being extravagant flattery of Queen Elizabeth. When the other characters kneel to Fortune in recognition of her power, Fortune points to the queen, saying, "There sits the Queene of chance, I bend my knees, / Lower then yours" (5.2.313–14). With this genuflection Fortune surrenders her authority to Elizabeth: "at thy chariot wheeles *Fortune* shall run, / And be thy captive and to thee resigne / All powers which heav'ns large patent have made mine" (ll. 318–20).

The other play featuring Fortune and performed before Queen Elizabeth near the turn of the century is *A Pleasant Comedy Showing the Contention between Liberality and Prodigality*, acted by the Chapel Boys at the Blackfriars theater in 1601 and at court on 22 February of that year; it was published in 1602. In all likelihood this is a revised version of a play performed by Paul's Boys at Christmas, 1567–1568. We don't know whether the representation of Fortune in the revised play differs from the original, but the anonymous playwright certainly accords Fortune considerable prominence.

As in *The Rare Triumphs* and *Soliman*, Fortune here wages a struggle for supremacy. In *Liberality and Prodigality*, however, Fortune's opponent is not Love or Death but the forces of goodness and rectitude.

Fig. 4: From John Lydgate's adaptation of Boccaccio's *Falles of...princes*, London, 1554 (cat. 11).

Vanity, the first character to appear onstage, announces the hostility between Fortune and Virtue: "'twixt their states, what difference will be, / Your selves shall judge, and witnesse when you see" (1.1.40–41).[22] That struggle is dramatized through the experience of characters who variously treat Fortune's son, Money. The playwright argues that the material things of life, conventionally regarded as the gifts of Fortune, must be handled prudently.

Liberality contains a few interesting details of Fortune's iconography. For example, Virtue, in characterizing her antagonist, reminds us that Fortune is sometimes depicted as literally two-faced:

She beares a double face, disguised, false, and fickle,
Full fraughted with all sleights, she playeth on the pack,

On whom she smileth most, she turneth most to wracke.

(1.3.117–19)

The double face suggests the deceptiveness of Fortune, her capacity to lull the unsuspecting into complacency.[23] Vanity may be speaking not only figuratively but also literally. That is, the actor playing Fortune may well have the image of a face attached to the back of his head. A two-faced Fortune had appeared in *Jocasta*, of course, as well as in the visual arts: for example, in John Lydgate's *Fall of Princes* (1554; cat. 11, fig. 4).

Fortune may also wear a blindfold (2.1.319), another traditional motif of the being who showers gifts upon the unworthy and withholds reward from the righteous. T. W. Craik points out that both Liberality and Prodigality call her "blind" (ll. 319, 909); moreover, "The fact that in this play she

descends from her throne unaided, and nearly strangles Prodigality when he attempts to break into her palace, need not prevent her eyes from being lightly bandaged, for in Bale's *Three Laws* provision is made for Moses' Law, blindfolded by the vices, to walk on and off the stage by himself" (p. 63).[24] If Craik is correct in his supposition, the blindfold may be decorated. In a narrative poem Michael Drayton describes Fortune's blindfold as "Painted about with bloody tragedies, / Fooles wearing crownes, & wisemen clogd in gives."[25] Of course, it would probably be difficult for a playgoer to discern such a pattern on a comparatively small piece of cloth. But if the image of "Fooles wearing crownes" were actually depicted on Fortune's costume, it would presumably have been visible to spectators. We know that Fortune's garment was sometimes decorated, for when the personification appears in Thomas Carew's *Coelum Britannicum*, a masque performed at Whitehall, 18 February 1634, "*the skirt of her garment [was] wrought all over with crowns, scepters, books, and such other things as express both her greatest and smallest gifts*" (ll. 624–26).[26]

The vivid stage action involving Fortune distinguishes the *Liberality and Prodigality* of 1601 from earlier Elizabethan treatments of Fortune. Even before we actually see the personification, Vanity alerts us to Fortune's magnificence: "Here will she mount this stately sumptuous throne" (1.1.30). When Fortune actually enters, the staging is especially impressive: "*Enter Fortune in her chariot drawne with kings*" (1.6.243–44.s.d.).[27] The song that follows this entry celebrates her power: "Reverence, due reverence, faire dames do reverence, / Unto this goddesse great, do humble reverence" (1.6.246–47). Because we do not know whether this staging was part of the original play in 1567–1568, we

cannot say with confidence that it inspired a scene in Christopher Marlowe's *Tamburlaine the Great*, performed c. 1587.[28] Marlowe dramatizes his protagonist's power and arrogance by this stage direction in *Part 2* of *Tamburlaine*: "*Enter Tamburlaine, drawn by the captive kings*" (5.3.41.s.d.). T. W. Craik, who suggests that Tamburlaine "is usurping Fortune's attributes," speculates on what led the author of *Liberality and Prodigality* to stage Fortune's entrance in a chariot: "it can be represented on stage far more easily than Fortune's wheel; it provides Fortune with a method of entrance; and it renders this entrance spectacular after the manner of those mobile pageants which appeared in royal entry processions and frequently employed allegory" (p. 96).

Following this entry Fortune ascends her throne, as Vanity earlier foretold. Later the playgoers see Fortune ensconced in her palace, though the theatrical company need not actually have constructed a set to represent the structure; the actors could have relied upon the imagination of the spectators to supply the particulars of the palace.[29] There must, however, have been a playing area above the stage, for an angry Prodigality climbs a ladder to "scale the walls" (l. 897).[30] This stage direction describes Fortune's response: "*Fortune claps a halter about his neck, he breaketh the halter & falles*" (ll. 903–4.s.d.). Whether Fortune bears any other hand prop we cannot tell from the script. And the description of Fortune's costume, while suggesting a sumptuous appearance, lacks specificity; Vanity announces that Fortune intends "t'appeare, / In her most gorgeous pompe" (1.1.26–27); later Fortune announces that she wears "vestures wrought with gold" (1.6.262). Possibly the garment worn by Fortune is multi-colored, for when she appears in a Jacobean masque, Robert

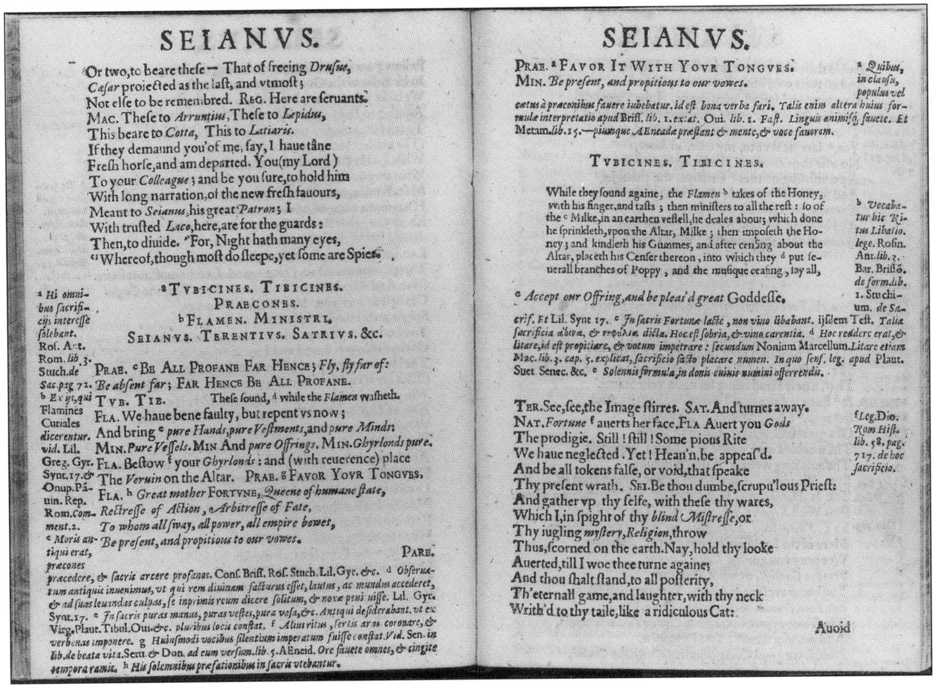

Fig. 5: From Ben Jonson, *Sejanus*, London, 1605 (cat. 6).

White's *Masque of Cupid's Banishment*, performed before Queen Anne at Greenwich in 1617, Fortune wears "a rich mantle wrought with changeable colours to expresse her incertainty" (ll. 249–51).[31] All we know for certain of Fortune in *Liberality and Prodigality*, however, is that she is winged, for, describing herself in the third person, she declares that "all the world doth hang upon her wing" (l. 958). If Fortune recedes in prominence as the forces of virtue gain hegemony, she has nevertheless created an impression of splendor through her chariot, throne, and palace.

Jacobean Staging

Fortune appears in several plays of the Jacobean era. The earliest of these is Ben Jonson's Roman tragedy *Sejanus His Fall* (cat. 6, fig. 5), first performed in 1603, according to the title page of Jonson's 1616 Folio. Although Fortune is not a speaking character, her statue appears near the end of the play and it has a crucial role in heralding the protagonist's demise. Several characters, including Sejanus, sacrifice at the altar of Fortune:

All. Accept our off'ring, and be pleased, great goddess.
Terentius. See, see, the image stirs!
Satrius. And turns away!
Natta. Fortune averts her face!
(5.184–86)[32]

Precisely what the statue looked like we do not know, though a cornucopia and rudder are the most common attributes of Fortune in ancient Roman statuary, as the learned

playwright must have known. We can be certain, however, that this statue was actually an actor whose makeup and costume were meant to suggest the color and texture of an inert statue. Without the illusion that a real statue stands before us, there can be no *coup de théâtre*. And as the text clearly indicates, the statue actually moves, turning away from the nonplussed Sejanus: "The statue does not simply swivel around, but—more effectively theatrically—turns only its head, neck, and torso away, so that Sejanus can mock it with its 'neck / Writhed to [its] tail, like a ridiculous cat.'"[33] In performance, then, an actor must represent Fortune.

The Valiant Welshman by R. A., first performed c. 1610–1615 by Prince Charles's Men, not only includes an onstage appearance by Fortune but also begins the dramatic action with her entry: "*Fortune descends downe from heaven to the stage*" (1.1.0.s.d.).[34] The stage direction suggests that the actor playing Fortune may have been lowered onto the stage with descent machinery, something that, so far as we know, was accomplished in no other play featuring Fortune as a character; it's also possible, however, that the descent was managed by means of a portable staircase from a playing area above. In any case that descent is meant to underscore her status as deity, one who can with a whim create either a tragic or comic conclusion in human events: "Thus from the high imperiall seate of Jove, / Romes awfull goddesse, Chaunce, descends to view / This stage and theater of mortall men" (ll. 1–3). Her role here is to summon harpers and they, in turn, by their music awake an ancient Welsh poet, who knows the story of Caradoc, the valiant Welshman of the play's title. The poet acknowledges Fortune's authority; he calls her "powerfull deity, / Arch-governesse of this terrestriall globe, / Goddesse of all

mutation man affords" (ll. 31–33). But nothing he says in the brief dialogue with Fortune offers a clue to Fortune's costume; nor do his remarks contain an indication that the actor playing the deity is equipped with any particular hand prop. Fortune herself mentions no detail of her appearance, except for a conventional reference to her smiles and frowns (ll. 11–12). The Welsh poet bids the playgoers "To keepe your understanding and your seates" (l. 83), and, with this entreaty, the action of the play proper begins. Later the poet returns to comment on the dramatized history, but Fortune, having exited in the opening scene, disappears from the play.

The last drama of the Jacobean era to create a character of Fortune is Thomas Middleton's *Hengist, King of Kent, or The Mayor of Queenborough*, first performed c. 1619–1620.[35] In the play's first scene the playgoers witness an elaborate dumb show. As indicated in the extant manuscripts of Middleton's play, the pantomimic action begins: "*ffortune is discovered uppon an alter, in her hand a golden round full of lotts*" (dumb show 1; ll. 1–2).[36] The quarto version of the play, published in 1661, makes it clear that the "round" is a ball.[37] The spherical object evokes that which Fortune customarily stands upon in the visual arts, and the lots, which the onstage characters proceed to draw and open, suggest the element of chance that lies at the heart of Fortune's meaning.[38] What remains unclear is whether the playgoers see on the altar a statue of Fortune made by an artisan or an actor costumed to resemble the deity in the manner of Jonson's *Sejanus*. Nothing in either the manuscript or the printed version of *Hengist* indicates that Fortune interacts with the various characters; and she speaks no lines.

R. C. Bald, the modern editor of this play, observes that "Middleton has evidently been

influenced by the accounts of the classical goddess Fortuna," especially of the temple dedicated to her at Praeneste, outside Rome; Bald goes on to cite Sir James Frazer's description of those who consulted the deity about the future: "The responses of the goddess were inscribed in archaic letters on oaken tablets, which were kept in a chest of olive wood. When anybody inquired of the oracle a boy thrust his hand into the chest, shuffled the tablets about and drew out one at haphazard. The writing on it purported to be the answer to the question."[39]

Middleton was not the first playwright to represent Fortune as a character bearing lots. In George Chapman's *An Humorous Day's Mirth*, acted by the Admiral's Men at the Rose theater in May-July 1597, a stage direction indicates the entry of a "*maid drest like Queene Fortune, with two pots in her hands*" (5.2.128.s.d.).[40] A boy who accompanies her explains that the pots contain "lots" (l. 174); characters proceed to draw their lots, which are two-line posies. Another instance of a character impersonating Fortune occurs in *Alphonsus, Emperor of Germany*, an anonymous play acted in its original form c. 1604 and acted in a revised version c. 1630–1631: "*Enter* Isabella, *the Empress;* Hedewick, *the Duke of Saxon's daughter, apparelled like Fortune, drawn on a globe, with a cup in her hand, wherein are bay-leaves, whereupon are written the lots*" (2.2.0.s.d.).[41] Like many another stage direction in Renaissance drama, this one is tantalizing: Was the actor sitting or standing on the globe? How large was the globe and how was it "drawn" onto the stage? And how exactly was the Duke of Saxon's daughter "apparelled" in her guise as Fortune? The surviving script reveals no answers to these questions.

To survey the plays in which Fortune becomes a character is to realize how limited

our knowledge of Elizabethan and Jacobean staging remains. Stage directions, alas, give us partial information at best about Fortune. The presence of hand props must usually be inferred from the dialogue. Rarely do we learn anything definitive about the costume of Fortune. Only *Jocasta* provides a detailed description of Fortune, and, as we have seen, that play, written for one of the Inns of Court, is atypical of London theatrical practice. What we can say is that when Fortune does become a character she creates a vivid spectacle, whether she arrives by chariot, on foot, or from the heavens. A wheel, wings, and blindfold are likely to be the most common features of Fortune on the stage. We learn, moreover, from both the dramatic action and dialogue that Fortune embodies the awesome power of circumstance to convert prosperity to misery, dejection to exultation. The plays we have examined afford ample evidence that Fortune's demeanor, words, and symbolic props signal her might, even if the precise details of her appearance onstage remain largely conjectural.

Notes

1. George Gascoigne and Francis Kinwelmersh, *Jocasta*, in *Early English Classical Tragedies*, ed. John W. Cunliffe (Oxford: Clarendon Press, 1912), dumb show preceding act 5.

2. Fortune's entry in a chariot may have been inspired by Petrarch's *Triumphs*, a popular work that, in illustrated form, depicts six personifications, each of whom rides in a chariot: Love, Chastity, Death, Fame, Time, Eternity.

3. Greg Walker, *The Politics of Performance in Early Renaissance Drama* (Cambridge: Cambridge University Press, 1998), 235.

4. W. Wager, *"The Longer Thou Livest" and "Enough Is as Good as a Feast,"* ed. R. Mark Benbow, Regents Renaissance Drama Series (Lincoln: University of Nebraska Press, 1967).

5. See Otto van Veen [Otho Vaenius], *Quinti Horatii Flacci Emblemata* (Antwerp, 1612), 155. This book, based on quotations from Horace, was first published in 1607.

6. T. W. Craik, *The Tudor Interlude: Stage, Costume, and Acting* (Leicester: Leicester University Press, 1962), 63.

7. Hans Sebald Beham's print of Fortune is dated 1541.

8. *An Edition of "The Rare Triumphs of Love and Fortune,"* ed. John Isaac Owen (New York and London: Garland, 1979).

9. John H. Astington, in *English Court Theatre, 1558–1642* (Cambridge: Cambridge University Press, 1999), observes of *The Rare Triumphs*: "The costumes in the play could have been quite elaborate,… and at court the actors are likely to have drawn on the resources of the Revels Office wardrobe store" (192). Astington goes on to list the large number of mythological figures in the play, including Fortune, and notes, "All of these appear either concurrently or in fairly rapid succession in act 1, and such a parade may have taxed the regular theatrical wardrobe of Derby's Men. For their Christmas performance [at court], they no doubt borrowed Revels costumes which may have been seen in other court shows on previous occasions."

10. *Soliman and Perseda* was entered in the Stationers' Register on 20 November 1592. The undated quarto was probably printed in the same year.

11. *"The Tragedye of Solyman and Perseda" Edited from the Original Texts with Introduction and Notes*, ed. John J. Murray (New York and London: Garland, 1991).

12. In Philip Massinger's *The Bashful Lover*, when one character says, "Fortune rules all," another answers, "We are her tennis-balls" (4.1.69). See *The Plays and Poems of Philip Massinger*, ed. Philip Edwards and Colin Gibson, 5 vols. (Oxford: Clarendon Press, 1976), vol. 4.

13. This arch, like the others in the coronation procession, was engraved by William Kip and published in Stephen Harrison's *The Arches of Triumph* (1604). For a brief but useful discussion of Kip's career as engraver, see Antony Griffiths, *The Print in Stuart Britain, 1603–1689* (London: British Museum Press, 1998), 41–45.

14. Reproduced in *Early German Masters: Jacob Bink, Georg Pencz, Heinrich Aldegrever*, ed. Robert A. Koch, *The Illustrated Bartsch* 16 (New York: Abaris Books, 1980), fig. 106 (396). The print is dated 1549.

15. Commenting on Dekker's presentation of Fortune, Cyrus Hoy, in *Introductions, Notes, and Commentaries to Texts in "The Dramatic Works of Thomas Dekker,"* 4 vols. (Cambridge: Cambridge University Press, 1980), cites Michael Drayton's description of Fortune in *Robert, Duke of Normandy* (1596): "Fortune wears about her neck a chain made of 'Princes crownes & broken scepters'" (1:95). There is, however, no indication in Dekker's stage directions that Fortune in *Old Fortunatus* wears such a chain.

16. *Old Fortunatus*, in *The Dramatic Works of Thomas Dekker*, ed. Fredson Bowers, 4 vols. (Cambridge: Cambridge University Press, 1953–1961), vol. 1.

17. Christopher Marlowe, *Tamburlaine the Great*, ed. J. S. Cunningham, The Revels Plays (Manchester: Manchester University Press; Baltimore: The Johns Hopkins University Press, 1981).

18. On this point, see my *Fortune and Elizabethan Tragedy* (San Marino, CA: The Huntington Library Press, 1983), 110–13.

19. Maarten van Heemskerck, for example, depicts Fortune, who is winged and wears a blindfold, holding a full purse in her right hand; in her left hand is a beggar's bowl. Reproduced by Ilja M. Veldman, *Maarten van Heemskerck and Dutch Humanism in the Sixteenth Century* (Maarssen: Gary Schwartz, 1977), fig. 59.

20. The stage direction points to the problematic relationship between Fortune and the three Fates. Because Fortune embodies chance and because the Fates signify that which is fixed, there is, logically, a distinction between Fortune and the Fates. Dekker, however, blurs that distinction by having Fortune tell Fortunatus, "I the worlds Empresse am, *Fortune* my name, / This hand hath written in thicke leaves of steele, / An everlasting booke of changelesse fate" (1.1.162–64).

21. Cyrus Hoy, in *Introductions, Notes, and Commentaries*, observes, "The three Destinies are presumably passing from one to another the thread of Fortunatus' life, which they will shortly terminate" (1:116).

22. *The Contention between Liberality and Prodigality, 1602*, ed. W. W. Greg, Malone Society Reprints (Oxford: Oxford University Press, 1913).

23. Fortune's two faces suggest a resemblance to the Vice of the interludes, who is metaphorically two-faced: Fortune and the Vice are both deceitful; they typically raise their victims to temporary prosperity, and they revel in the unexpected adversity that ensues (*Fortune and Elizabethan Tragedy*, 98). Significantly, Richard Southern, in *The Staging of Plays before Shakespeare* (London: Faber and Faber, 1973), observes that in *The Longer Thou Livest* "Fortune's opening lines are indeed more suited to a Vice than to a Lady" (477).

24. R. Mark Benbow, however, in his edition of *The Longer Thou Livest* argues that Fortune wears no blindfold "since she comments that the audience has not paid her proper homage" (note to l. 1037.1).

25. *The Tragical Legend of Robert, Duke of Normandy*, in *The Works of Michael Drayton*, ed. J. William Hebel, Kathleen Tillotson, and Bernard H. Newdigate, 5 vols. (Oxford: Basil Blackwell, 1931–1941), 1: 257 (ll. 115–16). The editors of Drayton's *Works* observe that "there appears to be no exact precedent for the chain and the painted veil" on Fortune's blindfold (5:39–40). In Drayton's poem, first published in 1596, Fortune and Fame tell the story of Robert, Duke of Normandy; these personified figures are antagonists, as they are elsewhere in Renaissance literature. In Thomas Kyd's *Soliman and Perseda*, for example, a character speaks of "cursed Fortune, enemy to Fame" (1.4.48).

26. *Coelum Britannicum*, in *Court Masques: Jacobean and Caroline Entertainments, 1605–1640*, ed. David Lindley (Oxford: Clarendon Press, 1995), 181. Carew's Fortune is also winged, carries a wheel, wears a blindfold, and has "her upper parts naked." Carew provides no explanation for the nakedness, but in the visual arts Fortune increasingly appears naked as she becomes identified with Occasion, and in this masque that conflation is evident: her head is described as "bald behind, and one great lock before" (l. 623). Implicit is the idea that the successful aspirant will grasp the forelock and thus gain prosperity.

27. Is this entry of Fortune in her chariot indebted to Gascoigne's example in *Jocasta*? It is difficult to know with any certainty since the original version of *Liberality* possibly antedates *Jocasta*.

28. It is possible that Marlowe's staging is indebted to *Jocasta* rather than to *Liberality and Prodigality*. Although Marlowe never saw a performance of *Jocasta*—he would have been two years old at the time of performance—he could have known the play in one of its printed versions. The play, with its dumb show of Fortune in a chariot, was included in Gascoigne's *A Hundreth Sundrie Flowers* (1573), *The Posies* (1575), and the *Works* (1587).

29. For a sixteenth-century woodcut of Fortune's castle, see John Doebler, *Shakespeare's Speaking Pictures: Studies in Iconic Imagery* (Albuquerque: University of New Mexico Press, 1974), pl. 14.

30. Samuel C. Chew, in *The Pilgrimage of Life* (1962; reprint. Port Washington, NY, and London: Kennikat Press, 1973), observes that Robert Allott, in *Wit's Theater of the Little World* (1599), "takes from Pausanias the information that at Mitylene there was a temple wherein was a ladder, 'a gift dedicatory to Fortune; signifying thereby that those that clymed up with ease Fortune favoured, and came headlong down if she frowned upon them'" (52).

31. "*Cupid's Banishment: A Masque Presented to Her Majesty by Young Gentlewomen of the Ladies Hall, Deptford, May 4, 1617*," ed. C. E. McGee, *Renaissance Drama* 19 (1988): 247. Robert White's description of Fortune also includes the information that Fortune has "a vaile before hir face to shew hir blindnes" (ll. 252–53) and a "wheele in hir hand to signify hir momentary favor" (ll. 255–58).

32. Ben Jonson, *Sejanus His Fall*, ed. Philip Ayres, The Revels Plays (Manchester: Manchester University Press; New York: St. Martin's Press, 1990).

33. Ibid., note to 5.186.

34. *The Valiant Welshman*, ed. Valentin Kreb, *Münchener Beiträge zur romanischen und englischen Philologie* 23 (Erlangen and Leipzig: A. Deichert, 1902). The play was entered in the Stationers' Register on 21 February 1615 and published in the same year.

35. The title page of the 1661 quarto indicates performance at the Blackfriars theater. *Hengist* is included in a play-list of the King's Men, 7 August 1641. According to Grace Ioppolo, in "Sexual Treason, Treasonous Sexuality, and the Eventful Politics of James I in Middleton's *Hengist, King of Kent*," *Ben Jonson Journal* 3 (1996), the play was written "between 1616 and 1620, revised by the author sometime before his death in 1627, and revised again by the King's Men before its first printing in 1661" (88).

36. Thomas Middleton, *Hengist, King of Kent; or The Mayor of Queenborough*, ed. R. C. Bald (New York and London: Charles Scribner's Sons [for the Trustees of Amherst College], 1938).

37. Ibid., note to the first dumb show.

38. Fortune's association with lots takes pictorial form in a painting by Dosso Dossi c. 1530–1542: Fortune holds a cornucopia and sits upon a transparent sphere while drapery billows behind her. Opposite her sits a male figure, who holds lots or lottery tickets in his hand and seems about to deposit them in an urn. This mysterious painting is reproduced in "Acquisitions/1989," in *The J. Paul Getty Museum Journal* 18 (1990): 173, fig. 10.

39. Bald, ed. *Hengist, King of Kent*, 103–4. Although the ancient statue of Fortune is long gone, the remnants of her temple may still be seen at Praeneste, known today as Palestrina. Situated at the top of a steep mountain, Fortune's majestic temple inspires awe even in its ruined state. And from the temple, which has been converted into a museum, the visitor looks out upon an astonishing vista of the valley below.

40. *An Humorous Day's Mirth*, ed. Allan Holaday, in *The Plays of George Chapman: The Comedies, A Critical Edition*, ed. Holaday (Urbana, Chicago, London: University of Illinois Press, 1970).

41. *The Tragedy of Alphonsus Emperor of Germany*, in *The Plays of George Chapman: The Tragedies*, ed. Thomas Marc Parrott, 2 vols. (1910; reprint. New York: Russell & Russell, 1961), vol. 2. Parrott includes *Alphonsus* in his edition of Chapman's tragedies because the 1654 title page attributes the play to Chapman. That attribution is not accepted today.

Controlling Fortune: The Moral Battle

"It is the mind that maketh good or ill,
That maketh wretch or happy, rich or poor."

(Edmund Spenser, *The Faerie Queene*, 6.9)

From the Stoics and Boethius, Christianity inherited the idea that the "slings and arrows of outrageous Fortune" (*Hamlet* 3.1) could be avoided by living a life of poverty, free of the demands and temptations of ambition, power, and pride. The particular qualities of Occasion and Nemesis that came to be added to the concept of Fortune also imply that an individual has the power to control his or her fortune. This belief is central to the elaborate and complex iconography found in emblems and on title pages and frontispieces throughout the Renaissance.

It is noteworthy that from the *Consolation of Philosophy* onward, the battle with Fortune is presented as being fought by an individual, not by a society. At the same time, contradiction and paradox are inherent in moralizing handbooks such as the *Mirror for Magistrates* that tell stories of the falls of great men to readers who are mostly not great men. The advocacy of moderation and even of poverty as ways to avoid good and bad fortune also discouraged "social climbing." Perhaps this is not surprising in a society with its origins in hierarchy but its present in the upward mobility that was a consequence of economic development, especially in large cities like London where the merchant class was growing, prospering, and demanding acknowledgement. Christian Humanism's belief in the power of wisdom and virtue, acquired through education, to avoid or conquer misfortune certainly gave the concept of individual responsibility a more practical foundation.

87.
Jean Jacques Boissard
Emblemes
Metz, 1595
No. LI: "Expers Fortunæ est Sapientia":
"Wisdom is free from Fortune"
See Astington, fig. 4

Fortune, holding a bag of what is probably gold, is the mast of a boat containing symbols of worldly goods; the unstable sea is contrasted with the land on which Wisdom sits with her symbols of learning, including an owl. Wisdom is in the foreground and on different land from that of the city in the background, towards which Fortune's boat is headed. The Greek on Wisdom's solid square reads, "Wisdom is a possession more prized than wealth." The verse can be translated,

The wise man has no need for prideful wealth,
Nor for other vanities that sustain the
   common man:
Inconstant fortune does not include
Prudent wisdom in her dubious craft:
Rather experience is her faithful hostess,
Who lodges her away from leisureful dwelling:

And whoever wishes to attain her must be
   studious,
Active and vigilant, enemy to laziness.

88.
Charles de Bouelles
[*Liber de sapiente*]
Paris, 1510
Page 116

On the left—the side of the world and the devil—sits Fortune. She is on a sphere at the edge of an open grave, elaborately dressed, blindfolded, and holding her wheel with its four figures. On the right—the side of God—sits Virtue represented by *Sapientia*, or Wisdom. She is on a block with her feet resting on a cushion, simply dressed, and holding a mirror, here the symbol of self-knowledge. The inscriptions on the two seats together read, "The seat of Fortune is round; the seat of Virtue is square," emphasizing the contrast between inconstancy and constancy. The "unwise man" above Fortune quotes Juvenal: "We make you a goddess, O Fortune, and place you in heaven"; the "wise man" above Wisdom says, "Trust to your Virtue;

Opposite: Detail from the title page of Sigismondo Fanti, *Triompho di Fortuna*, Venice, 1526 (cat. 95)

Fortune withdraws more quickly than the waves." Note the symbolic implications of the relative size of Fortune and the figures on her wheel.

89.
Pierre Coustau
Petri Costalii Pegma: cum narrationibus philosophicis
Lyons, 1555
Page 165: "Contra veteres, nullam Fortunam esse": "Contrary to the ancients, Fortune does not exist"

In this unusual emblem Fortune, with forelock, hangs from a rope, as does her wheel. The verse can be translated,

Behold how Rhamnusia [Nemesis] hangs on
*   our gallows*
And receives the punishment owed to her
*   wickedness*
She who once (may I say it) filled both
Sides of the account book, among the Gauls
*   paid the ultimate price.*
Why is the wheel of fickle Fortune of any
*   concern to you?*
What business does she have with you? You
*   will through yourself be wise.*

90.
George Wither
A collection of emblemes ancient and moderne
London, 1635
Book 1, no. 6: "Non Obest Virtuti Sors": "Fortune [luck] is not opposed to Virtue"

Here, as Wither's moralizing verse makes clear, the battle between Fortune and Virtue is being fought. The title page and the first twenty-one engravings of this copy of Wither were colored by a reader at some time in the past. The book has been extensively restored.

89

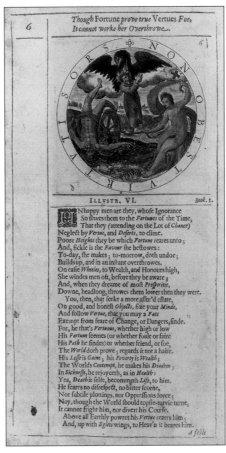

90

91

91.
Robert Recorde
The castle of knowledge
London, 1556
Title page

Blindfolded Fortune, holding a bridle, stands on an unstable sphere and with a cord turns "the Wheel of Fortune whose Ruler is Ignorance"; the wheel is inscribed, "Corruet statim qui modo scandit," which can be translated, "He who has just now climbed will immediately crash down again." Opposite is Urania, the heavenly muse, standing securely on a cube, holding a compass in one hand and in the other "the Sphere of Destiny whose Governor is Knowledge." The image of Fortune seen here also decorates the long gallery of Little Moreton Hall in Cheshire, England.

92.
Gilles Corrozet
Hecatongraphie
Paris, 1543
Sig. F7v

Fortune with her veil, on the sea, is poised with one foot on a dolphin, the other on a sphere, both symbolizing variability and change; in her hand she holds a broken mast. The winds blowing in each of the upper corners indicate that Fortune, like the sea, is constantly moving under their influence.

The verse below the picture emphasizes that Fortune comes when least expected and should not be trusted.

93.
Rembrandt van Rijn
The Ship of Fortune
Etching, from E. Herckman, *Der Zee-Vaert Lof*
Amsterdam, 1634
National Gallery of Art
Rosenwald Collection (1943.3.7092)

In the foreground on a fallen horse is the Emperor Augustus, who, having defeated Marc Antony at Actium, now gestures for peace to begin. In the left background is the Temple of Janus, the doors of which are being closed to signify peace, and in front of the temple is a statue of Janus. At the right, a group of merchant ships is setting sail,

VIRTVS · VOLVPTAS

TRIOMPHO DI FOR
TVNA DI SIGISMONDO
FANTI FERRARESE.

95

and the one just pushing off is guided by the goddess Fortune, who serves as the mast and holds the sail. Fortune here is acting in her role as the goddess of mariners and may symbolize the wind; the sail can be adjusted to her force by the men, putting them in control.

"Never think you Fortune can bear the sway, Where Virtue's force can cause her to obey."
(Queen Elizabeth I, "In Defiance of Fortune," in Puttenham, *Art of Poesie*)

94.
Principio Fabricii
Delle allusioni, imprese, et emblemi
Rome, 1588
No. CXXI: "Ars Fortuna Comes": "Fortune attendant on Art"

Fortune with winged feet, forelock, and razor stands on a horizontal wheel that moves on the sea like a whirlpool; she is paired with Mercury (Hermes), symbol of Art and Wisdom, who is on solid land, suggesting that Art can counteract the effects of Fortune, and that Art is not subject to chance.

95.
Sigismondo Fanti
Triompho di Fortuna
Venice, 1526
Title page

Fanti's *Triompho di Fortuna*, whose purpose is predicting the future, was published just before the sack of Rome in 1527. On the left of the title page, under the heading *Virtus*, is an attractive figure, probably *Bona Fortuna*; the crank she turns upward is attached to a globe with a zodiac band around it. On the right, under the heading *Voluptas*, is a malev-olent figure, probably *Malus Genius*, turning a crank downward. Both cranks are also held by Atlas, who carries the globe on his back. Atop this unstable globe is a Pope wearing the triple tiara, probably Clement VII; he is between two figures representing *Virtus*, pointing up, and *Voluptas*, pointing down. Standing on the left is a nude boy holding a large die, and kneeling in front of him is an astrologer holding a compass and astrolabe, probably Fanti himself. In contrast to the natural landscape on the right is a walled city, by implication Rome, with the Pantheon at the center and a large tower with a twenty-four hour clock and bell, signifying Time.[17] The message conveyed by this imagery is that neither Fortune nor Providence is in control of worldly events, and that the contest between the forces of good and evil continues.

96.
Antonio Fregoso
Dialogo de fortuna
Venice, 1521
Title page

Veritas or Truth gestures toward *Civitas Fortune* high on a rocky, forbidding hill; although all three men look back, the upheld hand of the first suggests a refusal to turn in that direction. The text is a philosophical poem in which Truth is presented as the only remedy against Chance or Fortune.

97.
Style of Vittore Gambello
Virtue and Fortune
Giuliano II de' Medici on obverse
Medal, bronze
National Gallery of Art
Samuel H. Kress Collection (1957.14.747b)
"Dvce Virtvte Comite Fortvna MDXIII":

97

"With Virtue as guide and Fortune as comrade 1513"

Virtue gives her right hand to Fortune. The implication of the symbolism is that such a position can be attained only by personal virtue combined with fortune. This medal was made in Rome after the election of the Medici Pope, Leo X, in March 1513.

98.
Jean Varin
Fortune chained to a chariot carrying Fame and France
Cardinal Richelieu on obverse
Medal, bronze
National Gallery of Art
Samuel H. Kress Collection (1957.14.10.b)
"Tandem Victa Seqvor": "Conquered at last, I follow"

The figure of France is seated in a chariot drawn by four horses; Fortune is chained to the chariot; and Fame stands on the chariot, guiding the horses and trumpeting.

99.
Francis Bacon
"Of Fortune"
In, *Essaies*, London, 1612
Pages 162–163

The main theme of Bacon's essay appears in the first few lines—that man is the maker of his own fortune, an idea Bacon expresses by giving a new twist to a conventional attribute of Fortune: "Therefore if a man look sharply and attentively, he shall see Fortune: for though she be blind, yet she is not invisible."

100.
Jean Baudoin
Recueil d' emblemes divers
Paris, 1638–1639
Vol. 2, page 454

Two cornucopiae, symbolizing Fortune, are joined with a caduceus and winged hat, representing Mercury, the god of eloquence, intellectual pursuits, and financial success: the benefits of the goddess come to those with the qualities of the god.

101.
Heinrich Oraeus
*Aereoplastes Theo-Sophicus, siue
Eicones mysticae*
Frankfurt, 1620
No. 61: "Patientia Triumphus":
"Patience triumphant"

In this engraving by Theodore Galle, a blind-folded Fortune holding a razor and a broken wheel is tied to the rear of a "Triumph of Patience." The wagon is being pulled by *Desiderium* (Desire) and *Spes* (Hope). In the margins the author cites various biblical passages. The verses below can be translated,

101

*Behold how splendidly Patience rides in her
    chariot
Drawn by Longing and ungrateful Hope.
Once powerful Fortune, her strength broken,
has yielded the place of honor to Patience
If you wish to conquer Fortune, learn how
    to endure.*

102.
Niccolò Machiavelli
The Prince
Translated by E. D.
London, 1640
Pages 208–209

for feare, and th'others for defire to recover the Kingdome of *Naples*; and on th'other part drew after him the King of *France*: for that King feeing him already in motion, and defiring to hold him his friend, whereby to humble the *Venetians*, thought he could no way deny him his fouldiers, without doing him an open injury. *Julius* then effected that with his violent and heady motion, which no other Pope with all humane wifdome could ever have done; for if hee had expected to part from *Rome* with his conclufions fettled, and all his affaires ordered before hand, as any other Pope would have done, hee had never brought it to paffe: For the King of *France* would have devifd a thoufand excufes, and others would have put him in as many feares. I will let paffe his other actions, for all of them were alike, and all of them prov'd lucky to him; and the brevity of his life never fufferd him to feele
the

the contrary: for had he litt upon fuch times afterwards, that it had been neceffary for him to proceed with refpects, there had been his utter ruine; for hee would never have left thofe wayes, to which he had been naturally inclind. I conclude then, fortune varying, and men continuing ftill obftinate to their own wayes, prove happy, while thefe accord together: and as they difagree, prove unhappy: and I think it true, that it is better to be heady, than wary: becaufe Fortune is a miftreffe; and it is neceffary, to keep her in obedience, to ruffle and force her: and we fee, that fhe fuffers her felfe rather to be mafterd by thofe, than by others that proceed coldly. And therefore, as a miftreffe, fhee is a friend to young men, becaufe they are leffe refpective, more rough, and command her with more boldneffe.

*I have confidered the 25 Chapter, as reprefenting me a full view of
humane*

In this section of his famous work, Machiavelli sets out his belief that Fortune can be controlled, and how to do it. His seventeenth-century translator then counters with his own view that Machiavelli's idea "cannot satisfie a Christian in the causes of the good and bad success of things." He quotes Ecclesiastes 9.5.11: "The race is not to the swift, nor the battle to the strong; neither yet bread to the wise, nor yet riches to men of understanding, nor yet favour to men of skill; but time and chance happeneth to them all." The translator particularly notes that even Machiavelli, as he himself admits, was not immune to bad fortune.

Controlling Fortune: Beating Fortune at her Own Game

"The future struggles not to let itself be mastered."

(Publius Syrus, *Sententiae*, no. 207, c. 43 B.C.)

That the ways of Fortune are uncertain and unpredictable has not prevented human beings from wanting to know the future. For as long as religions have advocated endurance and the acceptance of what comes, there have been astrology, palmistry, and other forms of fortune-telling. Today, predicting the future is big business, as any glance at a newsstand or telephone book will confirm, but we have merely inherited practices that originated in pagan antiquity. Those who are fortunate want to remain so, and those who are not want to become so: surely if we can know the future we can control it to our benefit? There have always been those who have made their own fortunes by exploiting this hope.

103.
Sir John Melton
Astrologaster, or, The figure-caster
London, 1620
Title page

The illustration of the astrologer with his paraphernalia is put into context by the subtitle of the book: "Rather the Arraignment of Artlesse Astrologers, and Fortune-tellers, that cheat many ignorant people under the pretence of foretelling things to come,…"

104.
Lorenzo Spirito
Le passetemps de la fortune des dez
Paris, 1637
Frontispiece

This book's subtitle is "Où chacun pourra veoir sa bonne où mauvaise Fortune." In the center of the frontispiece is a conventional image of Fortune on a wheel, on the sea, holding a sail; in each of the four corners are five sets of questions about the future and locations in the book to go for answers. At one stage in this process of seeing the future, dice are thrown.

105.
Giovanni Cipriano
A most strange and wonderfull prophesie vpon this troublesome world
Translated by Anthony Hollaway
London, 1595
Sig. B1r

The woodcut illustrates, "Tarquatus Vandermers seauen yeares study in the Arte of Magick, vpon the twelue [months] of the yeare, where many secrets are reueald vnto the world."

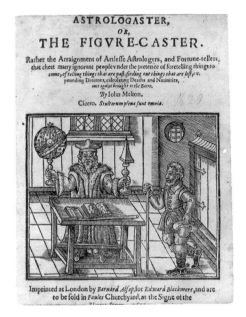

103

Opposite: From Robert Fludd, *Utriusque cosmi maioris*, Frankfurt, 1617–1621 (cat. 108).

Page left:

THE
Dutch Fortune-Teller, &c.

Vulcanus. 73.

2. THE Sick in Danger great doth lye,
Of this same present Malady;
The former Health which now is fled,
Will hardly be recovered.

3. OF any Thing which thou canst keep,
To raise thy Fortune, 'twill be Sheep;
Thou canst not have a better Thing,
Which will to thee more Profit bring.

4. TAKE heed, for if thy Secret be
Made known to Persons two or three,
It will no longer be conceal'd,
But unto many be reveal'd.

5. TO die a Maid you need not fear,
For many Children you shall bear;
'Tis three to one, e'er you be wed,
You will have lost your Maiden-head.

6. THOU art to have by Destiny,
Some Store of Husbands e'er thou die,
By which you may assured be,
The first will never bury thee.

7. A Merry Man, and diligent,
According to thy Heart's Content,
Will be to thee a Husband kind,
If thou canst get him in the Mind.

8. SO many Suitors you have now,
That very well you do not know
Which amongst them for to take,
Nor who you should your Husband make.

9. IF that thou shew thyself unkind,
When thou wouldst have him in the Mind,
His Heart will be against thee set,
That thou no more his Love shall get.

10. HIS Love is greater unto thee,
Than ever thine to him will be:
And if his Love should now decline,
The Fault is none of his, but thine.

11. YOU do not learned Men disdain,
But rather seek thereby to gain
Their Favours, or to be their Mate;
You do not bear them inward Hate.

12. FRIEND, to be short, and end the Strife,
Thou must and shall have but one Wife:
Make much and cherish her therefore,
For when she's dead, thou get'st no more.

B   *Luna.*

Page right:

Of all the QUESTIONS in General.

BA. 1. WHETHER the sick Body shall recover Health?
KI. 6. Whether what is said, be Truth, or not?
PV. 4. Whether you shall finish the Business well, you do purpose?
ZV. 7. Whether the Person who giveth you fair and good Words remains constant to you?
GA. 16. What your Dream may signify to you?
BK. 21. What Adventure you shall have this present Day?
ZA. 15. Whether you shall make a good and happy End?
FV. 2. Whether the Person who is gone to travel, shall come in good Health back again?
MA. 5. Whether you shall be welcome, and have kind Entertainment where you intend to come?
SL. 11. Who, amongst the married Couple, shall survive or outlive the other?
AR. 35. Whether you may trust your Secret to a Friend, or not?
DE. 3. Whether you shall perform your Journey?
XA. 8. In what Trade or Traffic you may have best Fortune to adventure your Estate or Money in?
ME. 20. To know if you shall soon come to Credit, Riches, Honour, and Preferment?
GE. 19. To know if it were good to keep private Intelligence, or Correspondence with such a one?
DA. 26. To know in what Kind of Cattle one had best Fortune to deal, or adventure withal?

Merry QUESTIONS for MEN and BATCHELORS, only, &c.

LE. 22. Amongst what Kind of People the Person may be best accepted of, and most beloved and respected?
RI. 27. How many Wives a Man shall be like to have?
GI. 25. What Manner of Wife he shall get?
ZE. 13. Whether you, at last, shall get those Things again, which you have formerly lost?
KV. 9. Whether the Person you think or imagine upon, doth mean truly with you, and respecteth you?
SO. 17. Whether that which you now think upon shall come to pass, yea, or no?
PO. 12. To know what Fortune may happen unto a Child newly born, either Boy or Girl?
XE. 14. To know whether you shall live long, increase in Riches, and be fortunate in your Age; yea, or no?
PI. 18. Whether it be good to pursue any further the same Business you desire to effect?
RE. 10. To know whether you shall follow the Counsel and Advice which is given unto you; yea, or no?
TE. 23. Whether she whom you love so dearly, and would fain have, doth likewise love you?
DA. 26. To know whether it be good and convenient to marry her whom you do intend?
XO. 24. To be certain, yea or no, whether yet you shall have her or not, whom you do respect and love?

For WOMEN and MAIDENS.

LO. 28. Amongst what People one may be accepted of?
FO. 34. To know whether you shall have any Children, yea or no, and how many?
BV. 31. If it were good and convenient to marry him whom you so constantly bear in your Mind?
LA. 32. What Husband may be allotted for you?
DO. 29. Whether he doth love you really and truly whom you love so constantly?
NE. 33. How many Husbands you shall have?
SO. 30. Whether you shall get him whom you do love?

The

106.
Ursula Shipton
The prophesie of Mother Shipton
London, 1641
Title page

"Mother Shipton" was a famous Yorkshire folk prophet who lived in a cave. She first came to be widely known with the printing of this pamphlet. The subtitle is "Fortelling the death of Cardinall Wolsey, the Lord Percy and others, as also what should happen in insuing times." The date of publication, at the beginning of another unsettled period in English history, is perhaps not entirely coincidental. She later predicted the Great Fire of London, which did occur; but she also forecast the end of the world in 1681. When that did not take place, it was predicted for the next year, and then the next, until no one believed her.

107.
John Booker
The Dutch fortune-teller
London, undated
Pages iv–5

This book includes tables and instructions on how to cast your own fortune, given in verses like the one on the left; on the right are the questions to be asked.

108.
Robert Fludd
Utriusque cosmi maioris
Frankfurt, 1617–1621
Vol. 2, section 2, part 4, title page
Illustrated page 88

In Theodor de Bry's engraving, an astrologer casts a chart for a man who wants to know the future. The open book on the stand on the right is not unlike Fludd's, full of charts and other symbols related to reading the stars. In the background is a symbolic sky in which sun, moon, and stars, the astrologer's primary tools, are all visible.

"**Wisdom still by seeing grows,**
But no man the unseen knows.
Shall he fare ill or well
Who of mortals can foretell?"
(Sophocles, *Ajax*, l. 1419–22, c. 409 B.C.)

109.
Joannes ab. Indagine
The book of palmestry and physiognomy
London, 1666
Sig. B2r

A hand with "The Table Line, or Line of Fortune" is one of the illustrations in this manual on fortune-telling. The fact that this is the sixth edition of this work indicates the popularity of such guides. In the "Epistle to the Reader" it is explained that,

the stars do not provoke or force us to any thing, but only maketh us apt, and prone: and being so disposed, doth as it were allure and draw us forward to our natural inclination. In the which if we follow the rule of Reason, taking it to be our only guide or governour, they lose all their force, power, and effect, which they by any means may have in and upon us. Contrariwise, if we give our selves over to follow our own sensuality and Natural disposition, they work even the same effect in us, that they do in bruit beasts.

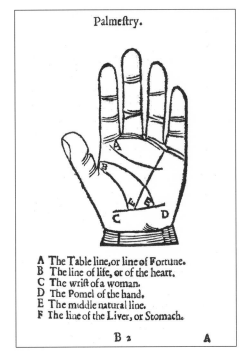

109

110.
Samuel Strangehope
A Book of Knowledge
London, 1679
Page 47

This woodcut is described on the facing page as "A Wheel of Fortune" which contains "the resolution of all manner of Questions, both for delight and satisfaction of the Reader." The top wheel, of "good fortune," shows three of the four conventional figures, one rising, one at the height of fortune, and one falling; the fourth, fallen figure is at the bottom of the lower wheel, of "bad fortune." The charts of numbers are necessary for the telling of a fortune. Over the page is a "catalogue of the Questions Resolved by this Wheel of Fortune."

111.

Jack Adams his perpetual almanack
London, 1662?
Frontispiece

The frontispiece shows Adams preparing a chart for the man in the lower corner as a woman behind him asks, "Pray sir, can you tell me my fortune." The subtitle advertises that the almanac contains "Astrological Rules & Instructions, Directing To an exact knowledge of all future things till the morrow after Doomsday." It is dedicated "To the Darling of Fortune John Late Lord Carleton a great Prince in Germany, Count of What-decallum, famous for his Prudence and Prowess, etc." As this suggests, Jack Adams's almanac is a parody of the real thing.

112.

Commonplace book
In Italian, c. 1700
Pages. 54–55

Of unknown authorship, this manuscript in Italian is probably largely a copy from another source. The purpose of the wheel is roughly translated: "To ascertain what will happen either good or its opposite to a person," and an example with instructions is given. The wheel is described as being associated with Solomon, Pythagoras, and Bede.

113.

Fortune-telling playing Cards
Fascimile of set printed in 1714

These are facsimilies of fortune-telling playing cards printed in 1714. The first such cards appeared about 1690; until then, regular playing cards were used to tell fortunes. Not surprisingly, few original sets of such well-handled items remain.

110

Magnifico Smokentissimo Custardissimo Astrologissimo
Cunningmanussimo Rabbinissimo Viro IACKO ADAMS
de Clarkenwell Greeno hanc lovelissiman sui Picturam

Hobbedeboody pinxit et ✂ ⚔ scratchabat

JACK
ADAMS
HIS PERPETUAL
Almanack,

WITH

Astrological Rules & Instructions,

Directing

To an exact knowledge of all future things till the morrow after Doomsday.

A

Work much desired and by great Providence preserved, and now published for the illumination of Posterity.

London, Printed for the Author and are to be Sold by the *Ginger-Bread* Woman in *Clarkenwell-Green*.

114.

Nostradamus

An almanach for the yere M. D. LXII

London, 1562

Nostradamus's prophecies, first published in 1555, are still known today. He said he received his prophecies as images which he then expressed as quatrains. Interpreters of these arcane verses believe that Nostradamus predicted cataclysmic events for the time just before and after 2000. The end of the world he said would come in 3797. Certainly his predictions were popular, as the condition and rarity of this fragment indicate.

115.

Jean de Meun

The Dodechedron of Fortune, or the Exercise of a Quick Wit

Translated by Sir W. B.

London, 1613

Sigs. B1v–B2r

This complex fortune-telling "game" takes the players through several steps before they reach the moralizing answers given in various categories related to love, marriage, rule, friendship, travel, health, etc.

116.

Anthony Copley

A Fig for Fortune

London, 1596

Title page

Copley's allegorical poem tells the story of "an Elizian out-cast of Fortune" who travels from despair to renewed belief in God's grace. Fortune is described as "A fickle Dame that commonlie misteemes / Those that her favours most of all importune" (B3r).

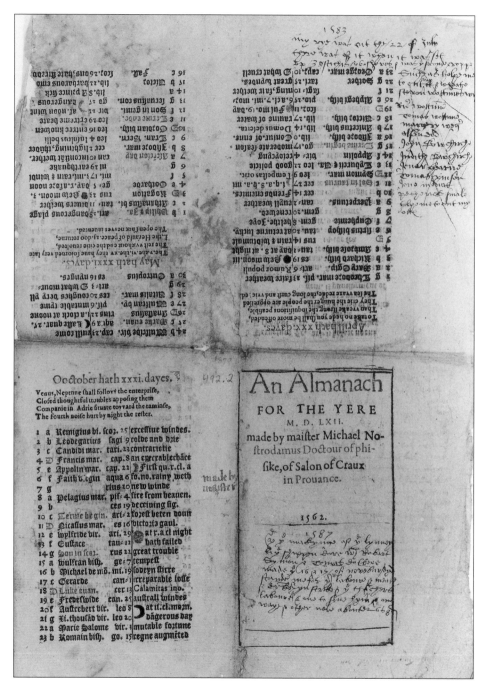

114

117.
Robert Daborne
A Christian Turn'd Turke
London, 1612
Sig. B1r

The beginning of this play undoubtedly captured the attention of the audience, who would have seen a group of men playing cards. As one refuses to continue playing, another tempts him, "Set but my hand out, heer's 400 Crowns vnlost yet, Fortune may make them yours." Another player, Gismund, exclaims, "Fortun's a Bitch, a meere strumpet, she hath turn'd vp the Ace so long, I haue ne'r an eye to see with, she hath sok'd me."

118.
Elizabeth I
By the Queene…by hir highnesse proclamation
and
A very rich lotterie generall [issued by the Privy Council]
London, 1567

In 1567 Queen Elizabeth authorized the first "Lotterie Generall," to raise money, as the Proclamation says, for "the reparation of the havens and strength of the Realme, and towardes such other publique good workes." The Proclamation also specifies that "The number of lots shall be foure hundredth thousand, and no more; and every lot shall be the summe of tenne shillings sterling onely, and no more." The first prize was "five thousande poundes sterling, that is to say, three thousande pounds in ready money, seven hundred poundes in plate gilte and white, and the rest in good tapissarie meet for hangings, and other covertures, and certain sortes of good linen cloth," as illustrated on the accompanying broadside.

119.
William Hogarth
The Lottery
Etching and engraving, 1721
National Gallery of Art
Rosenwald Coll. (1944.5.91)

Hogarth created an elaborate satire of the English national lottery, held between 1694 and 1826. The prizes were drawn in London's Guildhall. In the picture, the figure of National Credit presides over an allegory in which chance offers the paths of vice or virtue, represented by the various emblematic figures on the floor level. On the right side of the stage is blind Fortune, standing on her wheel, about to draw a lot from a large drum. This print, the first of a series by Hogarth, parodies Raphael's School of Athens and *Disputà*.[18]

120.
Crystal Ball on Stand
Glass crystal and wood
National Museum of American History
Smithsonian Institution

This crystal ball was owned and used by Patience Stanley Brewer (b. 1911), a member of a large Gypsy-American family.

121.
Tarot Cards
Facsimile of a set printed in the seventeenth century
National Museum of American History
Smithsonian Institution

These Italian tarot cards showing Fortune and Cupid are drawn from extant plates etched by Giuseppe Maria Mitelli.

Fig. 1: Cornelius Schut, *Neptune on the Sea and Fortune on a Sphere held by Occasio*, (cat. 39). Courtesy of the National Gallery of Art.

Spenser's "Wilde Fortune": Between the Forest and the Sea

Judith Dundas, *University of Illinois at Urbana-Champaign*

Two points in Spenser's prefatory letter to *The Faerie Queene* are relevant to a consideration of the role of Fortune in his epic. The first is that he has chosen "adventure" as his narrative mode to satisfy the desires of his readers, who for the most part "delight to read, rather for variety of matter then for profite of the ensample."[1] Describing the action of Book 1, he says that the Red Cross knight "went forth with her"—that is, with Una—"on that adventure." The third book, he tells us, has a knight, Sir Scudamore, unable to perform the adventure of rescuing his beloved Amoret from the vile enchanter Busirane and having to give up the task to Britomart. But in this book, there are, as well, "many other adventures intermeddled, but rather as accidents then intendments." The words "adventures" and "accidents" both imply Fortune and are the opposite of "intendments."[2] Spenser's choice of romance as his particular form of epic requires an apparent surrender to Fortune. By contrast with his passivity in the face of the adventures his characters encounter, Ariosto, the most influential of his epic-romance predecessors, exerts complete control over the world of his poem, including Fortune's whims.[3] Spenser can interpret what Fortune decrees but is seemingly powerless to intervene. His only means of imposing his will is suggested by his letter, which he concludes with mention of what may "seem tedious and confused" without the clarifying road map of the allegory.[4]

In explaining his method, Spenser more than once refers to "the general intention and meaning" of the poem. Here we have the antidote to Fortune as the presiding genius. Unaware of "the intentional fallacy" or of deconstruction, Spenser does not hesitate to explain his purpose, as well as the means by which he carries it out. The same opposites of Fortune and purpose are evident in the narrative itself, with a deliberate ambiguity about which prevails in human affairs. His knights and ladies are led by Fortune, even as they pursue their quest; but virtue alone, by the grace of Divine Providence, can succor them and lead them to their goal. Two landscape images in the poem represent the rule of Fortune: the forest and the sea. These with their natural symbolism transcend any narrow iconographic interpretation.

But before entering upon the world of *The Faerie Queene*, it is worth pausing to consider the role of Fortune in another of Spenser's narratives, his Ovidian poem *Muiopotmos*. Because the hero is a butterfly and cannot make decisions, right or wrong, the twin deities of Fortune and Fate preside over his destiny. Yet even the sad fate of Clarion in the spider's web is part of a divine plan: "It fortuned (as heaven had behight)"—this is how the poet introduces the negative presence of the spider in what might otherwise be the Garden of Eden. References to Heaven's decrees place the action in a divine perspective, even though the butterfly lacks the essential human characteristic of being able to make choices. His "cruell fate is woven even now / Of Joves owne hand" (235–36). As the entrapment of Clarion by Aragnoll, the spider, nears, the poet gives alternative explanations: "whether cruell Fate / Or wicked Fortune faultles him misled" (417–18). But from these abstract forces—"O sad hap and howre unfortunate!" (421)—he moves to the actuality, that an accidental blast of wind drove Clarion "Into the cursed cobweb, which his foe / Had framed for his final overthrow" (423–24). In Spenser's poem, chance is joined to malevolent plan—the spider's web—to bring about, inevitably, the butterfly's death.

The dangers that beset Clarion are like those that beset mankind in general: carelessness or recklessness can bring about death. The only safety lies in following divine guidance:

For thousand perills lie in close awaite
About us daylie, to worke our decay;
That none, except a God or God him guide
May them avoyde, or remedie provide.

(221–24)

These lines could well serve as a summary of the various actions in *The Faerie Queene*, with the difference that because the characters are human beings, not butterflies, they are able to make choices and listen to God. The butterfly of *Muiopotmos* can be only a partial symbol of the human soul as it daily confronts Fortune.[5]

Why does Spenser give Fortune a central role in his epic? He seems to see this pagan goddess, or the concept she represents, as descriptive of life here on earth but not as ultimately controlling human destiny. For this reason he offers alternative explanations for events: either Fortune or Divine Providence is responsible.[6] The one is from an earthly perspective, the other from the heavenly. It is an aspect of his fluidity of style and perception that he hovers between these explanations.

There is a minor but significant difference in the setting of Spenser's two narrative poems. Whereas Clarion meets his fate by wandering in a paradise garden, the heroes of *The Faerie Queene* journey through an uncharted forest; gardens are only enclosed spaces in that encompassing forest. The centrality of the forest as an image of a realm in which Fortune rules is brought home to us when Spenser sets the stage for the adventures of Red Cross and Una by their entry into the "wandering wood":

Led with delight, they thus beguile the way,
Untill the blustering storme is overblowne:
When weening to returne, when they did stray,
They cannot finde that path, which first was
      showne,
But wander to and fro in wayes unknowne.

(1.1.10)

In this wood, like all the woods of the poem, characters cannot find their way.[7] Here, the storm, itself an attribute of Fortune, underlines their helplessness. There is no escape from Fortune, whatever illusions of safety Una and Redcross cherish. Though every hero in the poem has a quest and a purpose, the difficulty is to know how to achieve that quest, what direction to take: "As in the woods, where in some places error leads wayfarers from the sure path, and this one goes off to the left, that one to the right, the same error leading them both astray, but in different directions"—so Horace describes the human condition.[8] The forests of medieval romance are the perfect metaphor for this uncertainty and for the apparent sway of Fortune in controlling human affairs.

If Spenser himself allows Fortune a certain role in the composition of his poem, in keeping with the illusion he creates that he does not know what will happen next, he also finds the forest a fitting image for the setting in which Sir Philip Sidney pursued his goal of fighting for Dutch independence:

It fortuned, as he that perilous game
In forreine soyle pursued far away:
Into a forest wide and waste he came,
Where store he heard to be of salvage pray.
So wide a forest and so waste as this,
Not famous Ardeyn, nor fowle Arlo, is.[9]

Even the fact that "forest" and "Fortune" share a syllable might have seemed to the Elizabethans to point to a link between the two concepts. Perhaps ironically, Shakespeare's *As You Like It* shows just the opposite interpretation: the Forest of Arden is represented as an escape from court life, where Fortune rules. Pastoral idealization supplies Shakespeare with an image of the forest as possessing the goodness of nature, at least in part.[10] A similar idealization colors the place where

Meliboe lives, in the adventure of Calidore in Book 6 of *The Faerie Queene*. Indeed, Calidore asks leave to "rest my barcke, which hath bene beaten late / With stormes of fortune and tempestuous fate, / In seas of troubles and of toylsome paine" (6.9.31). But of course that realm is shattered by brigands, much as Sidney's pastoral world in his *Arcadia* has the counter-balance of violence, both on the human and the animal level. In Sidney's own life, the forest, the scene of heroic endeavor, is no place of safety.

But the forest of *The Faerie Queene* is not only the realm of Fortune; it is also a dreamland. As a place where anything can happen, it permits a constant succession of adventures, answering readers' demand for variety. It also provides a unity of place for events that might otherwise be unrelated. When Rosemond Tuve said that Spenser's forest is more archaic than symbolic,[11] I think that she was referring to the imaginative basis of the allegory, which required a setting where chivalry could feel at home. This is not Dante's *selva oscura,* though the "Wandering Wood" or Wood of Error comes close to it. Nevertheless, Spenser, because his medium is romance, has literalized what remains metaphorical in *The Divine Comedy*.

Characters in the poem, whether good or evil, complain constantly of the blows Fortune has inflicted on them. But one moment Una is saying "Tempestuous Fortune hath spent all her spight" (1.7.25), and the next, good Fortune has brought Prince Arthur to her rescue: "At last she chaunst by good hap to meet / A goodly knight, faire marching by the way" (1.7.29). She asks: "But what adventure, or what high intent / Hath brought you hether into Faery Land?" (1.9.6). Arthur's reply sums up the mystery underlying both the events of *The Faerie Queene* and of *Muiopotmos*:

'Full hard it is,' quoth he, 'to read aright
The course of heavenly cause, or understand
The secret meaning of th' Eternall Might,
That rules mens waies, and rules the thoughts
*   of living wight.'*

(1.9.6)

Clearly, the forest harbors both *Fortuna Mala* and *Fortuna Bona*. Sir Mortdant, seeking adventures in order to prove his courage, happened upon the Bower of Bliss: "Him fortuned (bad fortune, ye may ghesse) / To come where vile Acrasia does wonne" (2.1.51). Good fortune, however, tends to suggest the workings of Divine Providence:

Providence heavenly passeth living thought,
And doth for wretched mens reliefe make way;
For loe! great grace or fortune thether brought
Comfort to him that comfortlesse now lay.

(3.5.27)

In the perilous state of the wounded squire of Prince Arthur, the appearance of Belphoebe is nothing short of a miracle. But Spenser likes the ambiguity of "grace or fortune" and often gives this alternative explanation of good events as if to leave unresolved the question of whether fortune rules or a divine plan controls what happens. In this way he can appear to suspend judgment, leaving his reader free to form his own opinion. It is the same kind of suspension of judgment, or indeterminacy, that characterizes the seemingly naive narrator and is thus part of the whole rhetoric of the poem.

If the forest is a place for testing virtue when it is confronted with evil fortune or when it has the good fortune of being rescued by divine grace, the pastoral world that Calidore enters in Book 6 at first appears to be safe from the whims of Fortune. Meliboe makes a confident Boethian statement:[12]

'In vaine,' said then old Meliboe, 'doe men
The heavens of their fortunes accuse,
Sith they know best what is the best for them…
'It is the mynd that maketh good or ill,
That maketh wretch or happie, rich or poore…
*   fooles therefore*
They are, which fortunes doe by vowes devize,
Sith each unto himselfe his life may fortunize.'

(6.9.29–30)

But this is part of the illusory peacefulness of the pastoral scene; it is too stoic a response to leave room for the action of divine grace. In the forest, on the other hand, knights must follow their destiny, even when they are not sure where to go. There is a goodness in submitting oneself to the pathless woods in the hope of ultimately finding and defeating the evil threat or of finding the unknown love. Clarion, the miniature hero who is really a pleasure-seeker in a garden, cannot represent the virtue of wandering. As a creature of instinct, he is totally under the control of fortune, whereas Spenser's knights may at least partially "fortunize" their lives, depending on their receptivity to divine grace.

Besides the pervasive forest of *The Faerie Queene*, there is another landscape image that represents the realm of Fortune. This is the more iconographically familiar one of the sea. While we do not expect to find the forest as an attribute of Fortune in emblem books or emblematic prints and pictures, the sea, ships, and wind readily illustrate this subject.[13] Because of long literary and pictorial tradition, these are immediately recognizable as identifying the characteristic instability of Fortune. An emblematic print by H. S. Beham (1541) shows Fortune with the typical wheel, ball, and a ship at sea, with sails billowing out in the wind (cat. 30; Kiefer, fig. 1).

Florimell, fleeing from the monster sent after her by the witch with whom she had

sought shelter, at last reaches the sea with the idea of drowning herself, but

It fortuned (High God did so ordaine)
As shee arrived on the roring shore,
In minde to leape into the mighty maine,
A little bote lay hoving her before.

(3.7.27)

Again, the alternative explanations of Fortune or God's Providence are offered as a way of keeping the reader in suspense about the outcome and also as a way of suggesting the mystery of what force governs the universe.

A little later, in the next canto, after a description of the False Florimell created by the witch to satisfy her son, we return to the adventures of the real Florimell:

But Florimell her selfe was far away,
Driven to great distresse by fortune straunge,
And taught the carefull mariner to play,
Sith late mischaunce had her compeld to
*   chaunge*
The land for sea, at random there to raunge:
Yett there that cruell queene avengeresse,
Not satsifyde so far her to estraunge
From courtly blis and wonted happinesse,
Did heape on her new waves of weary
*   wretchednesse.*

(3.8.20)

The whole stanza gives a picture of Fortune as controlling Florimell. Love has made her vulnerable. But the poet deliberately hides her eventual good fortune in being united with the beloved Marinell through her submission to the very sea from which Venus sprang. Proteus, who captures her and who threatens her with the same kind of seduction that also threatens Amoret at the House of Busirane, is but another aspect of Fortune in her changeableness.

So potent is sea imagery to describe love that Spenser brings his heroine Britomart

AMORVM.

Fig. 2: From Otto van Veen, *Amorum emblemata*, Antwerp, 1608.

And Fortune, boteswaine, no assuraunce knowes,
But saile withouten starres gainst tyde and winde:
How can they other doe, sith both are bold
    and blinde?'

(3.4.7–9)

This little allegory within the larger allegory of the book draws new vitality from the actuality of the sea setting and the uncertainty of Britomart's quest for her unknown love, Artegall. So conventional in its emblematic and Petrarchan origins, this passage shows Spenser's ability to infuse new life into even the most tired clichés; he has returned us to natural imagery to represent the instability of Fortune.

The boat of Britomart's emblematic complaint is literal in Guyon's voyage to the Bower of Bliss, "Where Pleasure dwelles in sensuall delights / Mongst thousand dangers and ten thousand magick nights" (2.12.1). The boatman, who may be *Virtus*, and the Palmer, who is Prudence, steer the boat among all kinds of hazards. On the journey, they see "a goodly" ship "laden from far with precious merchandize /… Which through great dis-saventure, or mesprize, / Her selfe had ronne into that hazardize" (2.12.19). As "the waves come rolling, and the billowes rore," the narrator speculates that "wrathfull Neptune" himself might be driving his whirling chariot this way, for there is not a puff of wind. A print by Cornelis Schut makes the same association between Neptune and Fortune (cat. 39, fig. 1). Even the description of the Whirle-poole of Decay suggests a wheel of Fortune:

Whose circled water rapt with whirling sway,
Like to a restlesse wheele, still ronning round,
Did covet, as they passed by that way,
To draw their bote within the utmost bound
Of his wide labyrinth, and then to have them
    dround.

(2.12.20)

down to the seashore to lament her lovelorn state, as many before her had done. Emblems such as Otto van Veen's of 1608 (fig. 2), and Petrarchan poetry, such as Sir Thomas Wyatt's (cat. 67), depict the lover as a ship at sea.[14] The difference in Spenser's use of the topos is that Britomart is actually sitting on the seashore when she compares herself to a boat adrift on the sea:

Tho, having vewd a while the surges hore,
That gainst the craggy clift did loudly rore,
And in their raging surquedry disdaynd
That the fast earth affronted them so sore,
And their devouring covetize restraynd,
Thereat she sighed deepe, and after thus
    complaynd.

'Huge sea of sorrow and tempestuous griefe,
Wherein my feeble barke is tossed long,
Far from the hoped haven of reliefe,
Why doe thy moyst mountaynes each on
    others throng,
Threatening to swallow up my fearefull lyfe?
O! doe thy cruell wrath and spightfull wrong,
At length allay…

For els my feeble vessell, crazd and crackt
Through thy strong buffets and outrageous
    blowes,
Cannot endure, but needes it must be wreckt
On the rough rocks, or on the sandy shallowes,
The whiles that Love it steres, and Fortune
    rowes;
Love my lewd pilott, hath a restlesse minde,

The schematic waves of emblem books are given the reality of physical danger in Spenser's description.

On the other hand, as Britomart, though not Guyon, will finally learn, the Venus who at one moment seems identified with *Fortuna Mala* may turn out to be *Fortuna Bona*:

Great Venus...
That with thy smyling looke doest pacifie
The raging seas, and makst the stormes to flie;
Thee goddesse, thee the winds, the clouds doe
*   feare,*
And when thou spredst thy mantle forth on hie,
The waters play...

(4.10.44)

The sea in its association with Venus provides a cosmic image of love as emerging from the destructive element of passion. Here the Lucretian hymn of praise serves to foreshadow all the lucky loves of the poem: Britomart's, Amoret's, Florimell's. The biform Fortune is essential to Spenser's conception of her role in human life, as she moves with what Rollenhagen calls "passibus ambiguiis."[15] The ambiguous references in *The Faerie Queene* to "grace or fortune" and other double explanations for events reflect this view of Fortune.

A parallel but contrasting figure to Britomart's image of herself as a boat buffeted by rough seas is Phaedria, the figure of Immodest Mirth, whom Guyon encounters on his way to the Bower of Bliss. She is a figure of Fortune, with no fear of Neptune or Jove:

'In this wide inland sea, that hight by name
The Idle Lake, my wandring ship I row,
That knowes her port, and thether sayles
*   by ayme;*
Ne care, ne feare I, how the wind do blow,
Or whether swift I wend, or whether slow;
Both slow and swift a like do serve my tourne;
Ne swelling Neptune, ne lowd thundring Jove

Can chaunge my cheare, or make me ever
*   mourne;*
My little boat can safely passe this perilous
*   bourne.'*

(2.6.10)

Her control of her boat contrasts markedly with Britomart's lament for lack of control, her pilot having "a restlesse mind." Phaedria, however, "knowes her port, and thether sayles by ayme."[16] Exempt from the true uncertainties of love and devoted only to the vice of sensual conquest, she lands Guyon, without his trusty guide, the Palmer, on her island that is a foretaste of the Bower of Bliss. In answer to his complaint that she has misled him and made him stray from his right course, she argues that she has brought him to a safe port, away from the perils of the sea (or, one might add, of the forest):

'Who fares on sea may not commaund
*   his way,*
Ne wind and weather at his pleasure call:
The sea is wide, and easy for to stray;
The wind unstable and doth never stay.
But here a while ye may in safety rest,
Till season serve new passage to assay:
Better safe port, then be in seas distrest.'

(2.6.23)

The temptation to rest is one that Calidore, the knight of courtesy in Book 6, will succumb to in the pastoral world, which seems a refuge from the heroic life of wandering in the forest: a safe port is the wished-for goal on land, as well as on sea.

The next canto of Book 2 is introduced with a seafaring analogy to illustrate Guyon's plight as he travels without the palmer but with a comforting, if not altogether reliable, sense of "his own vertues and praiseworthy deedes":

As pilot well expert in perilous wave,
That to a stedfast starre his course hath bent,
When foggy mistes or cloudy tempests have
The faithfull light of that faire lampe yblent,
And cover'd heaven with hideous dreriment,
Upon his card and compas firmes his eye,
The maysters of his long experiment,
And to them does the steddy helme apply,
Bidding his winged vessell fairely forward fly.

(2.7.1)

The image suggests Fortune's boat, but now with a man in charge. Ironically, Guyon is about to fall into the clutches of Mammon, an adventure from which he will barely escape. As so often in *The Faerie Queene*, a hero is inclined to be too confident of his own strength in dealing with Fortune. In fact, he is not so much in charge of his destiny as he likes to think.

Although human freedom is always limited by Fortune, new or modified attitudes to the goddess or concept in the Renaissance are reflected in Spenser's poetry. In *The Individual and the Cosmos in Renaissance Philosophy*, Cassirer remarks on "the new uncertainty" as signifying "a new liberation" as compared with medieval certainties.[17] Instead of the word "uncertainty," I would substitute, for Spenser, "fluidity." His imagination allows him to hold in solution not only all kinds of mythologies but also all kinds of beliefs. Hence Fortune the enemy is converted to Fortune the friend as the tester of loyalties, whether to truth, love, or any of the virtues celebrated in the poem. He does not introduce Fortune as an allegorical figure in the action because she must appear everywhere, under various guises, including time, mutability, and the innumerable figures of good and evil that turn up to mirror the realities of this life. Here we have been concerned primarily with two realms in which Fortune

holds apparent sway: the forest and the sea. They provide the setting for adventures, the unpredictable experiences that challenge the courage or *virtus* of the characters. By himself surrendering to the unpredictable, even as he pursues his purpose, Spenser matches his method to his theme and demonstrates the value of accepting the mutable and the unknown. There can be no security for his characters as long as they live. Mutability, a Fortune figure if ever there was one, is the poet's realm, as well as the realm of his characters.

If we consider, for purposes of comparison, Sidney's attitude toward fortune, it is clear he believes that the poet has a special role in showing the subordination of Fortune to Providence. In his *Apology for Poetry*, he distinguished between the poet and the historian as moralists by stating that the historian lets fortune "overrule the best wisdom" by his use of the "bare *was*," because he does not see the whole pattern in the apparently random effects of fortune.[18] At issue is divine justice, which the poet is obligated to reveal. The point is made in Philippe de Mornay's treatise, long associated with Sidney as translator: "that which is fortune to the foole, is none to the wise man: that which is fortune to the wise man, is none unto God. According to the measure of our knowledge or ignorance, so doth fortune increase or abate."[19] The poet, on the other hand, sets forth virtue "in her best colours, making Fortune her well-waiting handmaid, that one must needs be enamoured of her."[20] It is the same kind of argument that Pamela uses in her famous debate with the atheistic Cecropia: "Lastly, perfect order, perfect beauty, perfect constancy, if these be the children of chance, or Fortune the efficient of these, let wisdom be counted the root of wickedness, and eternity the fruit of her inconstancy."[21] Spenser would agree,

but he chooses a different narrative method from Sidney in, to some extent, aligning himself with the uncertainties of his characters, instead of maintaining the omniscient role of the narrator in the *Arcadia*.[22]

The sea assumes a new and important role in Book 5, the Book of Justice. The relationship between fortune and justice is examined through debates that Artegall, the knight of justice, is called upon to decide. The first of these is the argument of the giant who stands "Upon a rocke, and holding forth on hie / An huge great paire of ballance in his hand" (5.2.30). He boasts "That all the world he would weigh equallie." An example of the inequalities that he means to rectify is what the earth has taken from the sea and what the sea has taken from the land—the very complaint that Shakespeare voiced in his Sonnet 64, where he sees nothing but the triumph of time and mutability:

When I have seen the hungry ocean gain
Advantage on the kingdom of the shore,
And the firm soil win of the wat'ry main,
Increasing store with loss, and loss with store. . . .[23]

The giant, instead of accepting the inscrutability of Divine Providence and Fortune's role as a daughter of Justice, believes in his pride that he can correct all inequities. He is thus an example of False Justice. When Artegall tries to reason with him, that it would first of all be necessary to know what was the original state of things—something that no mortal can know—the giant replies:

The sea it selfe doest thou not plainely see
Encroch uppon the land there under thee;
And th' earth it selfe, how daily its increast
By all that dying to it turned be?

(st. 37)

Artegall uses the argument of the Garden of Adonis canto in Book 3 to state that "there is

nothing lost, that may be found, if sought" (st. 30). But arguments fail, and in the end, the iron man Talus, the agent of justice, shoulders the giant from his rock to be drowned in the sea (st. 49). A simile compares his fall to a shipwreck:

Like as a ship, whom cruell tempest drives
Upon a rocke with horrible dismay,
Her shattered ribs in thousand peeces rives,
And spoyling all her geares and goodly ray,
Does make her selfe misfortunes piteous pray:
So downe the cliffe the wretched gyant tumbled;
His battred ballances in peeces lay,
His timbered bones all broken rudely rumbled;
So was the high aspyring with huge ruine
  humbled.

(5.2.50)

The image of shipwreck is reminiscent of Fortune's wheel, which with a turn can bring down the mighty of the earth; the giant who had sought to level mountains is himself levelled.[24] Now Fortune as Nemesis serves Justice,[25] though this is not always her role. More often the storms of adversity threaten heroic endeavor or the smooth sailing of the lover.

Another instance in which Fortune is brought into relationship with Justice occurs in the story of the two brothers Amidas and Bracidas. Again the claim of the giant to overturn the decrees of Fortune is denied by the actions of the sea and Artegall's decision to abide by what the sea has given and what it has taken away. The sea took away from Bracidas part of an island he owned and gave it to his brother, Amidas, enlarging the latter's island. On the other hand, the sea gave to Bracidas a treasure chest that was originally sent to his brother as the dowry of the woman he was to marry. Bracidas claims that "what so good or ill / Or God or Fortune unto me did throw" (st. 14), he will

keep. Artegall's decree supports Fortune as instrumental to Justice:

'For what the mighty sea hath once possesst,
And plucked quite from all possessors hand,
Whether by rage of waves, that never rest,
Or else by wracke, that wretches hath distrest,
He may dispose by his imperiall might,
As thing at randon left, to whom he list.'

(5.4.29)

Even the randomness of the sea in its distribution of fortune must be accepted as part of a divine plan. That is to say, human conceptions" of justice must give way before the inscrutability of Divine Providence, which even Bracidas acknowledges when he speaks of "God or Fortune."

Both sea imagery and forest imagery are used in *The Faerie Queene* to describe Spenser's role as the storyteller who submits himself to Fortune.[26] Near the beginning and end of his epic, he describes himself as a voyager seeking safe harbor and the end of his journey. In the first instance, he marks the end of Book 1:

Now strike your sailes, ye jolly mariners,
For as we be come unto a quiet rode,
Where we must land some of our passengers,
And light this weary vessell of her lode.
Here she a while may make her safe abode,
Till she repaired have her tackles spent,
And wants supplide; and then againe abroad
On the long voiage whereto she is bent:
Well may she speede, and fairely finish
her intent.

(1.12.42)

Once again, Spenser refers to his "intent," just as he did in his prefatory letter. Only because he has an intention can he justify traveling on an unknown sea; otherwise chaos or Fortune would rule his art, rather than his pursuit of a goal under divine guidance.

The same point is made as he begins the last canto of the last book of *The Faerie Queene* that he completed:

Like as a ship, that through the ocean wyde
Directs her course, unto one certaine cost,
Is met of many a counter winde and tyde,
With which her winged speed is let and crost,
And she her selfe in stormie surges tost;
Yet making many a borde, and many a bay,
Still winneth way, ne hath her compasse lost;
Right so it fares with me in this long way.
Whose course is often stayd, yet never
is astray.

(6.12.1)

The emphasis on "never astray" is the measure of the importance Spenser attaches to his purpose even as he struggles to find his way on an uncharted sea. Although he seems to have followed Ariosto, at the beginning of the last canto of *Orlando Furioso*, in this metaphor of finally reaching the port, there is a new seriousness implied in the relationship between wandering and goal.

Spenser also uses forest imagery to describe his journey. After speaking of the delightful variety that beguiles his "weary steps" through fairyland, he offers up a prayer to the Muses:

Guyde ye my footing, and conduct me well
In these strange waies, where never foote
did use,
Ne none can find, but who was taught them
by the Muse.

(6.Pr.2)

The divine guidance needed to find one's way in the forest is as apt a metaphor for the poet as for any of the knights seeking to fulfil a quest. The knight of this last book, Sir Calidore, speaks to his predecessor, Sir Artegall, of the difficulty of finding his way to the Blatant Beast, which he must subdue:

'now I begin
To tread an endless trace, withouten guyde,
Or good direction how to enter in,
Or how to issue forth in waies untryde,
In perils strange, in labours long and wide,
In which although good fortune me befall,
Yet shall it not by none be testifyde.'

(6.1.2)

It is thus clear that the poet and his knights are bound on the same venture, at the mercy of fortune, unless divine guidance comes to their aid, as Artegall wishes for Calidore: "'Now God you speed… / And keep your body from the daunger drad'" (10). It was divine guidance that Clarion, in *Muiopotmos*, lacked. Then, too, the butterfly inhabited only a garden, whereas Spenser and his knights have the forest and the sea as their testing ground—far more challenging and pathless realms. With a goal or a quest, they are seekers after a shining light, to which neither good nor bad fortune can ultimately lead them, but only the virtue deep within their minds. To this extent, the poet shares the view of Meliboe, that each person may "fortunize," or make his own fortune; yet divine grace, or in the case of the poem, the Muse, is the only assurance that inner virtue will finally triumph over the vagaries of fortune.

The two kinds of form in *The Faerie Queene*, which I have elsewhere called expressive and restrictive,[27] correspond with the rule of Fortune and the purpose and plan of the poem. Plutarch, in his essay on Chance, is adamant that Chance or Fortune must not be allowed to have the dominant role in art.[28] Reason, or Athene, should always be in control. Similarly, in what sounds like a foreshadowing of some modern kinds of expressionist art, Cicero is critical of too much reliance on random effects: "It is

possible for paints flung at random on a canvas to form the outlines of a face; but do you imagine that an accidental scattering of pigments could produce the beautiful portrait of Venus of Cos?"[29] The same point is made by emblems that contrast art and fortune, such as Alciati's "Ars naturam adiuuans": Mercury, the god of rhetoric and patron of the arts, sits on a cube; Fortune sits on a ball (fig. 3). The epigram states: "Aduersus vim fortunae est ars facta" ("Art is made to counter the power of fortune").[30] Although Spenser seems to resemble his knights in their wanderings, as well as in their quests, he has a surer sense of direction than they have; that is, he sets his own bounds within which to wander. In the composition of his poem, art exercises a control over fortune that, in this life, may seem to be denied.

Again, Plutarch, commenting on a famous statue of Alexander the Great, asks, "Shall we admit, then, that greatness in a statue cannot, without the help of Art, be created by Fortune's profuse provision of gold and bronze and ivory and much rich material, but is it possible that a great man, or rather the greatest man of all that have ever lived, without the help of Virtue, was perfected through Fortune's supplying him with arms and money, foot and horse? But for him who has not learned how to use these things they are a danger, not a strength and enrichment, but a means of proving his weakness and pettiness" (*Moralia* 4:336). Fortune, then, cannot account either for art or for greatness, but, if properly used as opportunity, can contribute to both. To this classical formulation, Spenser, in recognition of human fallibility, adds the saving grace of faith in God.

The relationship of art to nature or fortune is also illustrated in an emblem with a little more action than the one already cited. Sambucus shows Mercury mending a broken

Fig. 3: From Andrea Alciati, *Emblemata*, Padua, 1621.

92   *Industria naturam corrigit.*

Ad D. H. Wh. patruelis mei F.

THE Lute, whofe founde doth moft delighte the eare,
  Was cafte afide, and lack'de bothe ftringes, and frettes:
Whereby, no worthe within it did appeare,
MERCVRIVS came, and it in order fettes:
    Which being tun'de, fuche Harmonie did lende,
    That Poëttes write, the trees theire toppes did bende.

Euen fo, the man on whome dothe Nature froune,
Whereby, he liues difpif'd of euerie wighte,
Induftrie yet, maie bringe him to renoume,
And diligence, maie make the crooked righte:
    Then haue no doubt, for arte maie nature helpe.
    Thinke howe the beare doth forme her vglye whelpe.

Ouid. Epift.14.

Si mihi difficilis formam natura negauit;
Ingenio forma damna rependo mea.

Infor-

Fig. 4: From Geoffrey Whitney, *A choice of emblemes*, Leiden, 1586.

lute, while a musician and a dancer perform nearby. Now the motto emphasizes industry as the corrective to blind nature: "Industria naturam corrigit." Whitney, using the same plate and motto gives his version (fig. 4):

The lute, whose sounde doth most delighte
  the eare
Was caste aside, and lack'de bothe stringes,
  and frettes:
Whereby, no worthe within it did appeare,
Mercurius came, and it in order settes:
Which being tun'de, suche Harmonie did lende,
That Poettes write the trees theire toppes did
  bende.

Euen so, the man on whome dothe Nature
  froune,
Whereby, he liues dispis'd of euerie wighte,
Industrie yet, maie bringe him to renoume,
And diligence, maie make the crooked righte:
Then haue no doubt, for arte maie nature
  helpe.
Thinke howe the beare doth forme her uglye
  whelpe.[31]

We are reminded of the rude force of Spenser's Mutablity as she tries to take over the heavens and is confronted by Mercury, sent down by Jupiter to the circle of the moon to learn what is disturbing her orderly activity. Defiant, Mutablity resolves "To set upon them [the gods] in that extasie; / And take what fortune time and place would lend" (6.23). Her alliance with fortune is unmistakable.

The relationship of Spenser's Fortune to his conception of nature is central to his Mutability Cantos, both through the speeches of Mutability and through the procession she calls up in support of her argument. The two places in nature considered here—the forest and the sea—are the particular domains of fortune, representing as they do wildness or

disorder. Yet in these last two cantos, mutability or change is viewed both as destructive of order and as contributing to the higher order of nature. There is a permanence that includes all the unpredictableness of fortune: "eterne in mutability" sums up this relationship. Perhaps it is only at the end of the poem, in these fragments of an unwritten book, that we are able to assess the universal role of fortune. Earlier complaints against her are reduced to their proper proportions, and this new perspective contributes to faith in an ultimate order, even if Spenser's final words in the two stanzas of canto 8 show a desire for an order outside nature:

Then gin I thinke on that which Nature sayd,
Of that same time when no more change
    shall be,
But stedfast rest of all things firmely stayd
Upon the pillours of eternity.
                                (8.8.1)

All human desire is concentrated here, at the end of a poem that explores both the power of fortune and its limitations. No single personification of this figure could embrace all the various aspects, but Mutability may be for Spenser the most inclusive representation. For all her political aspirations, she is placed squarely under the control of nature, the only power, apart from God, capable of controlling her wildness.

Nevertheless, the more positive interpretation, that Fortune can act as a guide, is fruitful in that it allows for the existence of a force other than reason to dictate how man should go. As Virgil, in *The Divine Comedy*, explains to Dante: "Your wisdom cannot strive with her. She foresees, judges and maintains her kingdom, as the other heavenly powers do theirs. Her changes have no respite. Necessity makes her swift, so fast men come to take their turn.... Happy with

the other primal creatures she turns her sphere and rejoices in her bliss."[32] She is like an angel turning her sphere. Often Dante alludes to the way fate or chance dictates the direction his journey takes. In a similar way, Spenser's characters are led by fortune to fulfil their destiny. Difficult though the path may be, they are guided inexorably to their goal. This view of fortune contrasts with the usual notion that the uncertainties of the Renaissance universe, coupled with a new emphasis on the individual will, resulted in the need to assert man's control over fortune and his own destiny. But fortune need not be the enemy, in opposition to virtue, if viewed as a minister of God. In that case, a wise passiveness is the best attitude, one that both Spenser and his characters have to learn to accept and that results in his turning a narrative tradition into the expression of a philosophical conviction.

Notes

1. All quotations from Spenser are taken from *The Complete Poetical Works of Spenser*, ed. R. E. N. Dodge (Boston: Houghton Mifflin, 1936). The prefatory letter is on pp. 136–38.

2. On the equivalence of Fortune and *Ventura* or *Aventure*, see Howard R. Patch, *The Goddess Fortuna in Mediaeval Literature* (Cambridge, Mass.: Harvard University Press, 1927), 39–40.

3. On this subject, see Robert M. Durling, *The Figure of the Poet in Renaissance Epic* (Cambridge, Mass.: Harvard University Press, 1965), chapter 5. See also his discussion of Tasso's attitude toward his epic material, chapter 6. Tasso's control over the shape of his poem coincides with his belief that the poet's relationship to his poem is analogous to God's relationship to the universe. Thus neither Ariosto nor Tasso provides a complete model for Spenser's narrator.

4. For further discussion of Spenser's letter, see my *The Spider and the Bee: The Artistry of Spenser's Faerie Queene* (Urbana, IL: University of Illinois Press, 1985), chapter 1. For a detailed discussion of Fortune in *The Faerie Queene*, see Michael Steppat, *Chances of Mischief: Variations of Fortune in Spenser* (Cologne: Bohlau, 1990). Steppat does not discuss Spenser's letter in the terms I use. He refers to the *virtus-fortuna* antithesis, rather than the *ars-fortuna* complementariness that I identify. Another difference in our approaches is that Steppat does not single out the forest of *The Faerie Queene* for particular discussion. He does not include it in his index, though he has several references to the sea as part of the iconography of Fortune.

5. In "*Muiopotmos*: A World of Art," *Yearbook of English Studies*, 5 (1975), 30–38, I discuss this point at greater length.

6. There is, of course, another explanation, as indicated near the end of Book 6. When the Blatant Beast frees itself from the iron chain with which Sir Calidore had bound it, this is attributed either to "wicked fate… or fault of men" (6.12.38). In contrast, the butterfly Clarion is specifically described as "faultles" (l. 418).

7. Angus Fletcher uses the image of the labyrinth to describe the symbolic importance of the forest in *The Faerie Queene*. See *The Prophetic Moment: An Essay on Spenser* (Chicago: University of Chicago Press, 1971). He does not relate the labyrinth directly to the rule of Fortune but does refer to it as "a necessary medium through which the hero must pass in his life of continuous initiation" (p. 36).

8. Horace, *Satires* 2.3, ll. 48–51, trans. Robert M. Durling, in *The Figure of the Poet in Renaissance Epic*, 165–66.

9. *Astrophel: A Pastorall Elegie*, ll. 91–96.

10. Shakespeare, of course, includes some of the negative aspects of life in the forest, such as Jaques' lament for the stricken deer.

11. Rosemond Tuve, *Allegorical Imagery: Some Mediaeval Books and Their Posterity* (Princeton, NJ: Princeton University Press, 1966), 380.

12. Cf. Boethius, *De Consolatione Philosophiae* (4, prose 7), trans. Chaucer: "For it is set in your hand…what fortune yow is levest (that is to seyn, good or yvel)." Book 6 has, according to Michael F. N. Dixon, twice as many allusions to Fortune as any of the other books. See his "Fairy Tale, Fortune, and Boethian wonder: Rhetorical Structure in Book VI of *The Faerie Queene*," *University of Toronto Quarterly*, 44 (1975), 141–65. See also the interesting discussion in Steppat, *Chances of Mischief*, 292–303.

13. The forest is actually a stage for the operation of fortune but it is not, like the sea, an image of Fortune in her changeableness.

14. Cf. *The Winter's Tale* 4.4. 496–572 (*The Riverside Shakespeare*, ed. G. Blakemore Evans et al., Boston, 1974), where Florizel speaks to Camillo of his tug of war with Fortune and of entrusting himself and Perdita to what the old lord calls "a wild dedication of yourselves / To unpath'd waters" (566–67). In Fig. 2, Cupid clings for dear life to a palm tree that symbolizes the strength and steadfastness of love amid the storms of adversity.

15. Gabriel Rollenhagen, *Selectorum Emblematum, Centuria Secunda* (Utrecht, 1613), no. 40.

16. The passage is modeled on Tasso, *Gerusalemme Liberata* 15.6.

17. Ernst Cassirer, *The Individual and the Cosmos in Renaissance Philosophy*, trans. Mario Domandi (New York: Harper & Row, 1964), 76.

18. Sir Philip Sidney, *An Apology for Poetry*, ed. Geoffrey Shepherd (1965; rpt., Manchester: Manchester University Press, 1973), 110.

19. Philippe De Mornay, *A Woorke concerning the trewnesse of the Christian Religion*, trans. Sir Philip Sidney and Arthur Golding (1587), 190.

20. *Apology for Poetry*, 111.

21. *The New Arcadia*, ed. Victor Skretkowicz (Oxford: Clarendon Press, 1987), 360.

22. Not writing in the tradition of chivalric romance, but rather of Greek romance, Sidney need not submit himself as writer to Fortune. Although his characters are constantly appraised in relationship to what Fortune sends them, Sidney, in contrast with Spenser, seems always to know what will happen next.

23. *The Riverside Shakespeare*, Sonnet 64, ll.5–8.

24. On this point, see Jane Aptekar, *Icons of Justice: Iconography and Thematic Imagery in Book V of "The Faerie Queene"* (New York: Columbia University Press, 1969), 38.

25. Jean Cousin, for example, in his *The Book of Fortune*, edited and translated by H. Mainwaring Dunstan (Paris and London: Librairie de l'art, 1883, pl. 131), refers to Fortune as the daughter of Justice. See also Richarde Linche, *The Fountaine of Ancient Fiction* (1599), sig. 2A4v. Thomas Carew, in his masque *Coelum Britannicum* (1634), has Fortune say that "since *Astraea* fled to heaven, I sit / Her Deputy on Earth, I hold her skales / And weigh mens Fates out" (ll. 687–89).

26. Jean Cousin, in his *The Book of Fortune*, has an emblem, No. 157, "Quod Ars Negat Fortuna Prestat" ("Fortune often produces what art cannot give"). The picture shows a ship with fishermen who are trying to use a net to catch fish. Meanwhile, a fish simply leaps into the ship without being caught in the net. Thus the art (not talent, as the translation says) of the fishermen in the form of the net is useless compared with fortune.

27. See reference in n. 4.

28. Plutarch, "Chance," in *Moralia*, trans. Frank Cole Babbitt (London: William Heinemann, 1928), vol. 2: 83–89.

29. Cicero, *De Divinatione*, I.13.12, trans. William Armstead Falconer (Cambridge, Mass.: Harvard University Press, 1938). But see Dio Chrysostom, the sixty-third discourse, for a reminder of the role that fortune can play in art. He alludes to the story of how Apelles, in despair over the difficulty of depicting the froth on the mouth of a horse, hurled his sponge at the painting, near the horse's bit: "And at the sight Apelles was delighted by what Fortune had accomplished" (*Discourses*, trans. H. Lamar Crosby [Cambridge, Mass.: Harvard University Press, 1985], vol. 5, 37). For further discussion of the subject, see H. W. Janson, "The Image Made by Chance in Renaissance thought," in *De Artibus Opuscula XL: Essays in Honor of Erwin Panofsky*, ed. Millard Meiss (New York: New York University Press, 1961), 254–66.

30. Alciati, *Emblemata* (Padua: Tozzi, 1621), 1c. The translation is from *Andreas Alciatus: The Latin Emblems*, ed. and trans. Peter M. Daly, Virginia Callahan, Simon Cuttler, Paola Valeri-Tomaszuk (Toronto: University of Toronto Press, 1985), l. 99.

31. Geoffrey Whitney, *A Choice of Emblemes and Other Devises* (Leiden: Plantin, 1586), 92. The Sambucus emblem appears in his *Emblemata* (Antwerp: Plantin, 1566), 52.

32. *Inferno* 7.85–97, trans. John D. Sinclair (New York: Oxford University Press, 1961), 103.

Notes to the Catalogue

1. *De Officiis*, trans. Walter Miller (London: William Heinemann Ltd.; Cambridge, Mass.: Harvard University Press, 1948), Book II, vi.

2. *Natural History*, ed. and trans. H. Rackham (Cambridge, Mass.: Harvard University Press, 1944), Book II, ch. v.

3. Information about the medals in the catalogue is from *Renaissance Medals from the Samuel H Kress Collection at the National Gallery of Art* (London: Phaidon Press, 1967).

4. Translated by J. A. B. (London, 1694), 421. Throughout this catalogue original spelling has been retained, but the "long s" and ligatures have not.

5. See Fern Rusk Shapely, *Catalogue of the Italian Paintings*, 2 vols. Washington, DC: National Gallery of Art, 1979, I: 481–82, II: pl. 342, 342a.

6. Quoted from Lily B. Campbell, *The Mirror for Magistrates*, edited from original texts in the Huntington Library (Cambridge: Cambridge University Press, 1938).

7. Unless otherwise indicated, information about engravings from the National Gallery of Art is taken from *Eva/Ave: Women in Renaissance and Baroque Prints*, H. Diane Russell with Bernadine Barnes (National Gallery of Art, Washington; Feminist Press at The City University of New York, 1990).

8. Frederick Kiefer, *Fortune and Elizabethan Tragedy* (San Marino: Huntington Library, 1983), 206–7.

9. Andrea Alciato, *Emblemata*, Lyons, 1550. Translated and annotated by Betty I. Knott with an Introduction by John Manning (Menston: Scolar Press, 1996), Introduction.

10. *Emblemata*, 133.

11. For a detailed discussion see Samuel Chew, *The Pilgrimage of Life* (New Haven and London: Yale University Press, 1962), 28–30.

12. For a detailed analysis of this engraving see Erwin Panofsky, "'Virgo & Victrix': A Note on Dürer's *Nemesis*," in *Prints: Thirteen illustrated essays on the art of the print selected for the Print Council of America* by Carl Zigrosser (New York: Holt, Rinehart and Winston, 1962), 13–38.

13. For a discussion of the "Table of Cebes" see Michael Bath, *Speaking Pictures: English Emblem Books and Renaissance Culture* (London and New York: Longman, 1993), 111–15.

14. Horace, *The Odes and Epodes*, with an English trans. by C. E. Bennett. Loeb Classical Library (London: Heinemann; New York: Putnam's Sons, 1939), 179.

15. Francis Yates, *Astraea* (London and Boston: Routledge and Kegan Paul, 1975), 49–50.

16. See John Pope-Hennessey, *Renaissance Bronzes from the Samuel H. Kress Collection at the National Gallery of Art* (London: Phaidon Press, 1965), 141.

17. Robert Eisler, "The Frontispiece to Sigismondo Fanti's *Triompho di Fortuna*," (*Journal of the Warburg and Courtauld Institutes* 10 [1947]), 155–59.

18. See Joseph Burke and Colin Caldwell, *Hogarth: The Complete Engravings* (New York: H. N. Abrams [n.d.]), no. 25, and David Bindman, *Hogarth and his Times: Serious Comedy* (Berkeley: University of California Press, 1997), 114.

Bibliography

Alciato, Andrea. *Emblemata*. Lyons 1550. Translated and annotated by Betty I. Knott with an Introduction by John Manning. Aldershot, England: Scolar Press, 1996.

Allen, Don Cameron. "Renaissance Remedies for Fortune: Marlowe and the *Fortunati*." *Studies in Philology* 38 (1941), 188–197.

Ashton, John. *A History of English Lotteries*. London: Leadenhall Press; New York: C. Scribner's Sons, 1893.

Bassein, Beth Ann. *Women and Death: Linkages in Western Thought and Literature*. Westport, Conn.: Greenwood Press, 1984.

Bath, Michael. *Speaking Pictures: English Emblem Books and Renaissance Culture*. London and New York: Longman, 1994.

Capp, Bernard. *English Almanacs 1500-1800: Astrology and the Popular Press*. Ithaca, NY: Cornell University Press, 1979

Cassirer, Ernst. *The Individual and the Cosmos in Renaissance Philosophy*. Trans. and Intro. by Mario Domandi. New York and Evanston: Harper and Row, [1964], rpt. 1972.

Chastel, Andre. *The Myth of the Renaissance 1420–1520*. Trans. Stuart Gilbert. Geneva: Editions D'Art Albert Skira, 1969.

Chew, Audrey. *Stoicism in Renaissance English Literature*. New York: P. Lang, 1988.

Chew, Samuel. *The Pilgrimage of Life*. New Haven: Yale University Press, 1962.

Cicero, *De Officiis*. Trans. Walter Miller. London: William Heinemann Ltd.; Cambridge, Mass.: Harvard University Press, 1948.

Cioffari, Vincenzo. *Fortune and Fate from Democritus to St. Thomas Aquinas*. New York, 1935.

___. "Fortune, Fate, and Chance." In *Dictionary of the History of Ideas*. New York: Charles Scribner's Sons, 1973.

___. "The Function of Fortune in Dante, Boccaccio, and Machiavelli." *Italica* 24 (March 1947), 1–13.

Clements, Robert J. *Picta Poesis: Literary and Humanistic Theory in Renaissance Emblem Books*. Rome: Edizioni de Storia e Letteratura, 1960.

Cochrane, Rexmond C. "Bacon and the Architect of Fortune." *Studies in the Renaissance* 5 (1958), 176–195.

Cotgrave, Randall. *A Dictionarie of the French and English Tongves*. London 1611. Facsimile by Da Capo Press, Amsterdam, New York, 1971.

Diehl, Huston. *An Index of Icons in English Emblem Books 1500–1700*. Norman and London: University of Oklahoma Press, 1986.

Elton, William R. *King Lear and the Gods*. San Marino: Henry E. Huntington Library, 1966; rpt. Lexington: University Press of Kentucky, 1988. Chapters 2 and 3.

Eva/Ave: Women in Reniassance and Baroque Prints. H. Diane Russell with Bernadine Barnes. National Gallery of Art, Washington; Feminist Press at The City University of New York, 1990.

Ewen, C. L'Estrange. *Lotteries and Sweepstakes*. London: Heath Cranton, 1932.

Farnham, Willard. *The Medieval Heritage of Elizabethan Tragedy*. Berkeley: University of California Press, 1936.

Flanagan, Thomas. "The Concept of *Fortuna* in Machiavelli." In *The Political Calculus: Essays in Machiavelli's Philosophy*. Ed. Anthony Parel. Toronto: University of Toronto Press, 1972.

Fowler, W. Warde. "Fortune." In *Encyclopedia of Religion and Ethics*. Ed. J. Hastings. New York, 1914.

___. *Roman Ideas of Deity in the Last Century before the Christian Era*. London: Macmillan, 1914. Pp. 78–79.

Freeman, Rosemary. *English Emblem Books*. London: Chatto & Windus, 1948.

Guarino, Guido A., trans. *The Albertis of Florence: Leon Battista Alberti's "Della Famiglia."* Lewisburg: Bucknell University Press, 1971.

Hinks, Roger. *Myth and Allegory in Ancient Art*. London: The Warburg Institute, 1939. Pp. 76–83.

Kiefer, Frederick. *Fortune and Elizabethan Tragedy*. San Marino: Huntington Library, 1983.

Miedema, Hessel. "The Term *Emblema* in Alciati." *Journal of the Warburg and Courtauld Institutes* 31 (1968), 234–250.

Mosley, Charles. *A Century of Emblems*. Aldershot, England: Scolar Press, 1989.

Nelson, Alan H. "'King I Sit': Problems in Medieval Titulus Verse." *Mediaevalia* 8 (1982), 189–210.

___. "Mechanical Wheels of Fortune, 1100–1547." *Journal of the Warburg and Courtauld Institutes* XLIII (1980), 227–233.

Panofsky, Erwin. "'Virgo & Victrix': A note on Dürer's *Nemesis*. In *Prints: Thirteen illustrated essays on the art of the print selected for the Print Council of America* by Carl Zigrosser. New York: Holt, Rinehart, Winston, [1962], 13–38

Patch, H. R. *The Goddess Fortuna in Medieval Literature*. Cambridge, Mass., 1927; rpt New York: Octagon Books, 1967.

___. *The Tradition of Boethius*. New York, 1935; rpt Russell and Russell, 1970.

___. "The Tradition of the Goddess Fortuna in Roman Literature and in the Transitional Period" and "The Tradition of the Goddess Fortuna in Medieval Philosophy and Literature." *Smith College Studies in Modern Languages* 3 1922), April, 131–235; July, 179–232.

Pickering, F. P. *Literature and Art in the Middle Ages*. London: Macmillan, 1970. Figs. 1a, 8b, and pp. 168–222.

Pitkin, Hanna F. *Fortune is a Woman: Gender and Politics In the Thought of Niccolo Machiavelli*. Berkeley: University of California Press, 1984.

Pliny. *Natural History*. Ed. and trans. H. Rackham. Cambridge, Mass.: Harvard University Press, 1944. Book II, ch. v.

Pomeroy, Sarah B. *Goddesses, Whores, Wives, and Slaves: Women in Classical Antiquity*. New York: Schocken Books, 1975.

Rawski, Conrad H., ed. *Petrarch's Remedies for Fortune Fair and Foul*. 5 vols. Bloomington and Indianapolis, 1991.

Robinson, David M. "The Wheel of Fortune." *Classical Philology* 41 (1946), 207–216.

Scribner, R. W. *For the Sake of the Simple Folk: Popular Propaganda for the German Reformation*. Cambridge: Cambridge University Press, 1981.

Steppat, Michael. *Chances of Mischief: Variations of Fortune in Spenser*. Koln: Böhlau Verlag, 1990.

Tervarent, Guy de. *Attributs et Symboles Dans L'Art Profane 1450–1600*. Geneva: E. Droz, 1958; rpt 1997.

Trompf, G.W. *The Idea of Historical Recurrence in Western Thought from Antiquity to the Reformation*. Berkeley and Los Angeles: University of California Press, 1979.

Van Marle, Raimond. *Iconographie de L'Art Profane*, vol. 1. La Haye: M. Nijhoff, 1931. Pp. 178–202.

Wittkower, Rudolph. "Chance, Time and Virtue." Chap. IV in *Allegory and the Migration of Symbols*, London: Thames and Hudson, 1977.

Index to Books, Manuscripts, Engravings, and Objects in the exhibition